Post-pandemic Urbanism

Doris Kleilein / Friederike Meyer (eds.)

jovis

Doris Kleilein / Friederike Meyer (eds.)

Post-pandemic Urbanism

jovis

Intro

"We will not wake up in a new world after the lockdown; it will be the same, just a little worse." With these words, the French writer Michel Houellebec was looking ahead, even in May 2020, to the time after the pandemic. Today, somewhere between the third and fourth wave, it is not yet possible to say when the aftermath will begin or whether we will have to live with the ups and downs of this and other pandemics in the long term. The extent of the social upheavals will probably only become apparent in the coming years. The pandemic is polarizing: is it nothing more than a nightmare from which we hope to wake up as quickly as possible? Or a wake-up call to more decisively address the many crises facing us (first among them climate change)? The city is both a stage for, and an indicator of, social processes. The fact that everyday urban life can change fundamentally within a few days is the collective, at times unsettling, experience we have gained from the pandemic.

For this book, we asked urban planners along with scholars in the fields of urbanism and architecture, most of whom come from Europe, to venture a view of the post-pandemic city. Working from home, undertourism, online shopping: what will remain after the pandemic and to what extent? What are the implications for planning and living in cities? What opportunities will the pandemic bring to finally address familiar urban development problems while putting the common good first? The results are essays and conversations, analyses, and a series of images. The fourteen contributions are both speculative and challenging. The majority of the authors do not believe that urbanity is in crisis, as has been repeatedly claimed since the outbreak of the pandemic. On the contrary: they are united by a constructive search for what makes cities resilient to coming disasters.

Phineas Harper and Maria Smith begin with a dialog about degrowth. Against the backdrop of the pandemic, they explore why construction is so anchored in the paradigm of economic growth, while making the connection between social and environmental issues and calling for an architecture of sharing.

Home offices and online shopping have swept city centers that have remained empty for months: what will become of the city centers if they are no longer a place where people shop and work? Seeing the pandemic as a boost for new retail concepts, Felix Hartenstein outlines a radical new start for city centers and considers what other reasons there might be to go into town. Agnes Müller shows what will happen when employees no longer commute to the company every day: coworking spaces, currently the topic of so much discussion, could not only function as business models but also revitalize neighborhoods and establish themselves as a third place between the home and the corporate office.

Nowhere was the quality of life in cities during the pandemic more evident than in public spaces. Aglaée Degros, who advised the city of Brussels on new mobility concepts and social participation after the outbreak of the pandemic, argues for the upgrading of the immediate living environment; together with Sabine Bauer and Markus Monsberger she identifies traffic space as the area that needs to be redistributed (including on the outskirts of the city). David Sim draws initial conclusions from a study of the use of public spaces in Danish cities by Gehl during (and after) lockdown; arguing in the Scandinavian democratic tradition, he calls for a return to simple, local solutions and a city of short distances.

In the research project "Urban Obsolescences," which began even before the pandemic and is now receiving increased attention, Stefan Rettich investigates how new uses and fields of transformation are constantly emerging even in densely built-up cities. Will we no longer need department stores, office buildings, or airports in the future?

Not only metropolitan areas, but also many small and medium-sized cities are beginning to change as a result of the pandemic. Together with Sascha Anders and Stephan Große, Thomas Krüger outlines recent developments in rather unspectacular places in Germany that have long been out of the focus of urban research and are now suddenly, at least in some regions, becoming attractive again. The surge in digital working could become a driving force in the development of rural areas: Doris Kleilein sees collaborative projects for living and working as the harbingers of a new way of living in the countryside.

Some municipalities are already facing up to fundamental trans-formation processes, as becomes clear in the conversation with Anke Butscher and Bárbara Calderón Gómez-Tejedor about the growing movement of the common good economy. Butscher and Gómez-Tejedor use German and Spanish examples to explain the instrument of public good accounting: what framework must a municipality set if it truly wants to act sustainably and for the good of all?

Avoiding the overburdening of public health systems was high on the agenda of pandemic responses worldwide. Friederike Meyer examines the role of temporary hospitals and shows how the pan-demic could permanently alter hospital planning and future sites of convalescence.

Philipp Stierand points out the weaknesses of urban food systems, arguing that the coronavirus pandemic has collided with the pandemic of diseases caused by civilization that has been rampant for decades. He calls for a new food policy so that cities are safely and locally supplied with healthy food and food poverty can also be combated in Germany.

Cities have always been places not only of coexistence but also of exclusion. Ananya Roy uses Los Angeles as an example to describe the effects of racist urban planning and housing policies that became more acute during the pandemic. But it is not only in the United States that COVID-19 has hit the less privileged particularly hard. Given the multiple crises facing cities, from housing short-ages to gridlock to the spread of disease, Tatjana Schneider calls for more participation and equity in planning and a re-politicization of planning processes.

The collective Non Voyage investigates how the frenzied standstill of the pandemic could affect tourism infrastructure. Using familiar imagery from social media, advertising, and art, the authors dissect the elements of the tourism industry, analyze the desire to consume other cultures, and prescribe a rehab cure for a society addicted to travel.

The new normal: the term became a buzzword for the uncertain, ever-changing nature of everyday life during the pandemic. But how new is the new and how normal the normal? The pandemic has shown that cities need structural changes to prepare for future crises, especially climate change. This book is intended to encourage forward-thinking in the ongoing exceptional situation. It is an invitation not only to endure or consume the city, but to help shape it.

More than Enough!

A Dialog on Degrowth and the COVID-19 Disaster

Degrowth is an economic theory proposing a designed reduction of resource consumption in wealthy societies to bring net human activity in line with planetary limits while lowering inequality and nurturing cultural and ecological flourishing. For decades, many environmental economists, philosophers, and artists have been exploring the functional and aesthetic possibilities of an economy that is no longer reliant on endless growth, but rarely have those ideas been tested on the urban landscape. In 2019, the Oslo Architecture Triennale, a Norwegian architecture festival titled "Enough: The Architecture of Degrowth," put degrowth at the heart of its curatorial agenda, with a program of performance, science fiction, and installations exhibiting many architectural and spatial proposals for what degrowth could mean for contemporary cities. Here, two of the Triennale's chief curators, engineer and architect Maria Smith and critic Phineas Harper, reflect on degrowth in the light of the COVID-19 catastrophe and ask why architecture seems so rooted in a paradigm of infinite economic expansion.

Phineas Harper: The first case of COVID-19 was recorded on November 17, 2019, one week before the conclusion of the Oslo Architecture Triennale. The Triennale's participants sought to imagine a society with almost no aviation; in which workers spent less time commuting and more time at home; in which cities embraced walking and cycling, and the complex, high-carbon consumerism of wealthy societies gave way to low-impact pastimes— reading, board games, DIY, handicrafts, gardening, and long walks. The Triennale imagined a world in which mutual aid networks proliferated as greenhouse gas emissions and gross domestic product fell. We pondered radical change, confident that it wouldn't happen. Meanwhile, the arrival of a novel coronavirus ensured a vast economic contraction, and a distorted form of degrowth is already on its way.

The global disaster of COVID-19 is, of course, nothing like degrowth. Degrowth proposes a sociable culture, bursting with festivities and collectivity, and, crucially, lower inequality, whereas the fight against COVID-19 has for many brought crushing isolation, techo-dependence, and more inequity. But are there glimmers of hope to salvage from the tragic pandemic? We've seen that some societies have adapted with phenomenal vigor, proving a capacity to change for the common good that agents of the high-carbon status quo claimed was impossible. We've seen huge drops in aviation and other polluting practices. Forced to adopt a new normal, many have seen more clearly the deep flaws of the old normal. However, we've also witnessed the speed with which the privileged few who benefit from economic growth have fought to resume the destructive state of affairs that was halted by COVID-19. Will future generations look back on the pandemic as a bitter but vital course correction, or another missed wake-up call?

Maria Smith: It's true that there are some cosmetic similarities between the more romantic qualities of a degrowth culture and the weird quarantine life many have been forced to embrace, but let's be clear—though economies are contracting, this pandemic is no degrowth. Financial support has been distributed unevenly, leaving many in extreme poverty, and public transport is shuttered. Stockpiling and hoarding have indicated a sinister pull away from that centerpiece of degrowth: sharing. However, I agree that we have seen unprecedented action taken across the public, private, and volunteer sectors, proving that the scale of change required to avert climate breakdown and adopt a radical new economy is possible. COVID-19 could be a pivot point in our transition to a socially and environmentally just society.

For this to happen, however, I believe it's critical to acknowledge that the pandemic is itself a product of anthropogenic ecological breakdown. The ever-increasing demand for resources—from sneakers to smartphones to skyscrapers—is driving the invasion of landscapes to mine rare materials, build infrastructure, and exploit the land for unsustainable intensive agriculture. These demands are degrading

ecosystems and forcing species into strained new relationships with each other, increasing the likelihood of pathogens
jumping from species to species, including humans. Unsustainable land and resource use has exposed humanity to
the heightened risk of pandemics like COVID-19. Unless the
underlying causes are addressed, there will be more.
It's appalling that it's come to this—that wealthy economies need
such a terrible wake-up call, comprising a death toll of more
than one million people. What can be done to make sure wealthy,
polluting societies really take action now so that it doesn't require
another pandemic or another after that to finally effect change?

PH: I think architects have a huge responsibility. Little contributes
more to global heating than the making and running of buildings.
Any efforts to fight climate change will fail without radically
reforming how architecture and cities are designed and cared
for. Faced with this enormous hurdle, many feel paralyzed. Some
architects even worry that climate change heralds the end of their
craft—fearing that new construction standards will be so stringent
that any capacity to express joy, tectonics, or civic values through
architecture will be crushed under the weight of regulations. I
disagree. I think this moment is extraordinarily exciting as much as
it is scary, and that it could, if we embrace it, push architecture to
be more enmeshed with living processes, and more nurturing of
vivacious cultural expression and a flourishing natural world. I don't
see a problem too difficult to address within our current paradigm—
I see an opportunity to change that paradigm.

Practicing architecture in the face of climate breakdown
means huge changes in the way we build, the materials we
work with, the care we provide for the urban fabric, and the
kinds of buildings, infrastructure, and neighborhoods we
create. There's never been a more exhilarating time to practice architecture. But where to start?

MS: Start with what exists already. Waiting for futuristic technology to save the day is mistaken and dangerous. For example,
take the hype surrounding carbon capture technology in the early
2000s. The idea that vast forests could draw carbon out of the
atmosphere then be burned for energy while intercepting and
burying the newly emitted CO_2 was so attractive but ultimately
didn't come at the speed and scale required. The 2018 IPCC report
was in part so shocking because this idea—that carbon capture
would ride in on a white horse—was revealed to be a fantasy.

The good news for architects is that we already have the technologies to address the emissions associated with our industry. We have timber, stone, and earth. We know how to reuse existing buildings, how to insulate with natural materials, manage internal environments with heat pumps and heat recovery systems, and how to manage moisture alongside heating, cooling, and ventilation.

The problem isn't that we don't know how, but that we aren't doing it—not nearly enough. Why aren't architects acting?

PH: Agreed. Mao Zedong was born in an earth house. The childhood home of Walter Raleigh was made from a mix of earth and straw. Wilhelm Wimpf built one of the tallest rammed earth buildings in the world in Weilburg, Germany—where it still stands, two centuries after completion. Of all the cultural, architectural, and urban UNESCO World Heritage Sites, more than 160 were built with earth. For ten millennia, earth has been one of the most widely used construction materials on, well, Earth. Yet despite its vanishingly small carbon footprint, earth is almost absent from contemporary architecture. Young architects today are rarely being tutored in how to design with adobe, cob, or rammed earth. Instead, in wealthy societies in particular, most architects specify a narrow catalog of highly processed, high-carbon materials like concrete, steel, and cement (which alone accounts for 7 percent of global carbon-dioxide emissions), often achieving poorer results.

Take concrete versus stone. Limestone has a compressive strength of 200 N/mm² and produces fairly low emissions, since stone can be quarried and shaped with relatively little energy. But we rarely use limestone raw. Instead, we turn it into concrete, an incredibly energy-intensive process involving grinding, heating, crushing, sintering, quenching, granulating, blending, and casting. We're left with a material that now has a compressive strength of just 40 N/mm². All that energy for a weaker material! Why?

The answer can in part be found in how we measure the value of an economy: gross domestic product (GDP). GDP principally measures economic activity. More economic activity in a country means a rising GDP, which is what economists call growth and what most governments prioritize. Concrete has high emissions because the processes that go into making it are complex. This is bad for the planet but good for GDP, as at every stage of the concrete manufacturing process materials, labor, and energy must be traded. Over time, complex GDP-boosting but ecologically harmful materials like concrete are incentivized in growth-pursuing economies, with huge industries building up around their use, while simple materials like earth or stone are disincentivized.

Those who uncritically pursue GDP growth will always make poor decisions about how and from what to build. But what would a society no longer chasing GDP growth be like? Other than a renaissance in low-impact construction materials, what possibilities could be unlocked in an economy in which GDP was designed to shrink?

MS: A degrowth economy could unlock a positive, reciprocal relationship between humanity and the environment. In seeking to grow the economy more every year, we cause huge damage to habitats.

Endless extraction has made it almost impossible to even imagine that humans, particularly in the West, can ever live in harmony with nature. Scraps of land designated as a nature reserve or a national park salve the conscience of polluters but reinforce the artificial division between humans and nature. The truth is that a world in which humanity is part of a thriving natural ecosystem is possible, but it's become difficult for many of us to conceive of. Describing her botany students, Robin Wall Kimmerer says: "They are well schooled in the mechanics of climate change, toxins in the land and water, and the crisis of habitat loss … [but] they cannot think of any beneficial relationships between people and the environment … Perhaps the negative examples they see every day—brownfields, factory farms, suburban sprawl—truncated their ability to see some good between humans and the earth … How can we begin to move toward ecological and cultural sustainability if we cannot even imagine what the path feels like?"[1]

The pursuit of economic growth has not only driven the extraction and exploitation of Earth's resources; it has excused it. This twisting of ethics to suit an economic project is one of the growth paradigm's most toxic legacies.

PH: The quest for growth has incentivized the exploitation of not just nature but other humans for centuries, fueling colonial imperialism and subjugation. A precursor to GDP was conceived in the

1   Robin Wall Kimmerer, *Braiding Sweetgrass: Indigenous Wisdom, Scientific Knowledge and the Teachings of Plants* (London: Ingram, 2015).

seventeenth century to finance the Commonwealth of England's invasion of Ireland. Oliver Crowell, a military leader in the 1648–49 English Revolution, took out loans to fund his Parliamentarian army, promising he'd repay lenders with land taken from the Irish. To do this, Cromwell employed the economist William Petty to assess the value of all Irish land in the 1655–56 "Down Survey," taking into account natural resources and profitable output. The linking of economic activity to political territory, today the basis of GDP, has roots in English colonialism.

In his 2016 BBC "Reith Lectures," philosopher Kwame Anthony Appiah further argues that the modern idea of racial difference was concocted to morally excuse the conquest and enslavement of peoples across the Global South for economic gain by European colonists. "Many historians have concluded that one reason for the increasingly negative view of the Negro through the later eighteenth century was the need to salve the consciences of those who trafficked in and exploited men and women."[2]

For Appiah, European imperialists constructed elaborate lies of racial differences in pursuit of expanding their economies in order to justify their heinous crimes, co-opting the sciences and humanities of the day: "One illustrious discipline after another was recruited to give content to color. And so, in the course of the nineteenth century, out of noisy debate, the modern race concept took hold."[3] The pursuit of expansion has birthed many monsters; racialization, fueling and fueled by inequality, is among its most vulgar spawn.

Degrowth is therefore, for me, not just an ecological movement but an anticolonial and antiracist one. But I find the wider climate movement sometimes skirts or ignores social issues entirely. Think of Extinction Rebellion's absurd claim to be "beyond politics," for example.

MS: Too often, social and environmental issues are pitted against each other. Degrowth economists argue that climate breakdown exacerbates global inequality and vice versa, but many in the West believe taking climate action impinges on personal freedoms. This egocentric view fails to acknowledge the enormous inequality of freedom entrenched by current socioeconomic systems. For example, under international climate accords, countries report

2   Kwame Anthony Appiah, "Mistaken Identities," BBC Radio 4 "The Reith Lectures," https://www.bbc.co.uk/programmes/b081lkkj, last accessed August 19, 2021.
3   Ibid.

emissions on a territorial basis. Nations only register emissions that occur within their borders. In line with this system, wealthy nations are not held responsible for the carbon emitted in making the energy, cars, smartphones, or steel beams they consume, so long as those goods are manufactured offshore. This makes the emissions of Western economies seem smaller, and artificially inflates the ecological impact of the Global South. Under contemporary climate accords, the Global South is both more likely to suffer the effects of climate and ecological breakdown and be disproportionately blamed for it. Taking meaningful climate action does not curtail net freedom, but only the high-carbon culture of the wealthy West.

Economic growth is often naively credited with single-handedly improving the quality of life of billions, but the real picture is more nuanced. As Jason Hickel points out in Less Is More, a study by Chhabi Ranabhat and others showed that the greatest predictors of improved life expectancy are sanitation and universal healthcare. These collective infra-structures aren't a direct result of economic growth but rather of progressive political movements, and the "historical record shows that in the absence of these forces, growth quite often worked against social progress, not for it."[4] To expand the freedoms of the many, then, there may be some limits on the freedoms of the few: namely, the freedom to exploit others and the freedom to curtail the freedoms of others.

PH: Limits on the freedom to live in energy-inefficient homes connected by car-dominated motorways. Limits on the freedom to make tedious commutes to sedentary office jobs. Limits on the freedom to mass-farm animals. Limits on the freedom to cram into budget airline cabins and travel at enormous speeds to fleeting foreign holidays. How many of the freedoms promised to the citizens of wealthy societies are really worth fighting for?

At one level, degrowth is simply a recognition of physical re-alities. It's increasingly clear that there's a direct link between greenhouse gas emissions and economic growth. In fact, in the past two decades, the only year net carbon emissions fell was 2009—the same year the world economy shrank. Even if growth could be decoupled from emissions, there's an energy problem, because energy consumption rises with GDP. A 2 to 3 percent growth rate seems very small but in fact means

4   Jason Hickel, *Less Is More: How Degrowth Will Save the World* (London: William Heinemann, 2020).

energy consumption doubles around every three decades.
At that rate, within a few centuries, Earth will need to harness 100 percent of the 174 petawatts of solar energy that reach it to power its economy. In less than two-thousand years, Earth will need to harness the entire energy output of the Sun! It's simply impossible for the economy to infinitely double, just as it's impossible for energy consumption to infinitely double. At another level, degrowth offers a radical critique of what we value and why. If we were less hooked on growth, what more substantial freedoms would we fight for? What about a freedom from the tyranny of work that could allow time to revel in economically unproductive but culturally rich pastimes? What about a freedom from efficiency that would allow time to travel slowly but well, enjoying rewarding journeys in good company rather than making a high-carbon dash for one's destination? What about the freedom from the solitary servitude of domestic labor in nuclear-family housing incentivized in many wealthy economies? What could freedom from growth unlock?

MS: Degrowth could bring shared luxury, joy, and, perhaps most preciously, time. Time to care for ourselves, each other, and our environment. As Barbara Smetschka and her fellow researchers reported in their 2019 study into the carbon footprint per hour of different activities (in Austria), some of the lightest carbon activities are sports, socializing, reading, resting, and volunteering.[5] A move to an economy within planetary limits would bring more time for so many of the things that make life worth living, from romance to music to amateur sports tournaments to transformative justice reading groups.

Degrowth could free time from the enormous and damaging labor of erecting monstrous new buildings, used not for housing but for profit. Instead, time could be spent on the restoration of habitats. This could include the reclamation and reconfiguration of buildings and materials to meet collective needs. The architecture of a degrowth future won't be the polished, finished gleam of sci-fi films, but more the charming eclecticism of a cherished and much-mended vintage heirloom dress worn with a high-performance raincoat: the best of every technology brought together. This

5   Barbara Schmetschka, Dominik Wiedenhofer, Claudine Egger, Edeltraut Haselsteiner, Daniel Moran, Veronika Gaube: "Time Matters: The Carbon Footprint of Everyday Activities in Austria," 2019, https://doi.org/10.1016/j.ecolecon.2019.106357.

architecture will require an ongoing tinkering and will come with a new attitude to maintenance and repair.

PH: When caring for your body, you don't go on one huge jog at the turn of each decade and then sit on the couch for the following ten years. From exercising to cleaning to nutrition to relationships, regular small acts of care are superior to occasional big bursts of activity punctuated by prolonged periods of neglect. Yet many commissioners of contemporary buildings seem chronically averse to repair commitments. Choices in material specifications are regularly made solely to reduce maintenance needs, frequently at the cost of higher environmental impacts. Building with thatch and earth, for example, has almost negligible emissions, but architects today rarely specify these traditional materials, on the grounds that they require periodic repair.

I'd argue that this harmful preference for longevity over periodic maintenance is driven in part by the desire to make architecture a form of economic asset. Building owners make a connection between the solidity of a building's fabric and the stability of its financial value. But designing with long-lasting high-carbon materials that require little repair but generate enormous emissions in their production is a false economy.

MS: This is the payday loan of architecture. Investing large amounts of energy in construction in the short term suffers from the high-carbon intensity of our current energy grid (which, according to Our World in Data, globally runs on only around 10 percent renewables). It also neglects the many other impacts an extractivist architecture has on the environment. The stability of our ecosystem relies on the rhythm of cycles: the water cycle, carbon cycle, nitrogen cycle, and many more. Sustainable architecture should sync into these cycles without overwhelming them, extracting materials for construction only at a pace that can be regenerated. We must move past this idea of creating an architecture that's a finished, final, inert product and embrace an architecture in sync with ecosystem processes.

PH: The making of new architecture is often called "regeneration" but frequently couldn't be further from it. New construction is typically called for when neighborhoods are perceived to have fallen into decline and development is rolled in, in order to turn things around. Yet often, the new facilities simply replace those that once existed but have been neglected, closed, or relocated over preceding decades, indelibly scarring communities with each cycle of demolitions. Far better would be a culture of maintaining buildings, facilities, and social infrastructure continuously, constantly caring for places and their people.

MS: Language is part of the problem. The term "regeneration" suggests positive renewal, but its use in architecture often masks violent destruction. The term "sustainability" is similarly misleading and is often used to describe practices that merely moderate environmental harm rather than promoting positive outcomes. Organic farming, for example, as it is commonly practiced in Europe and the United States, moderates the harmful use of pesticides but is often more water intensive and land intensive. Reusable cups moderate the harm of pollution stemming from single-use plastics but consume far more energy to manufacture and clean, ultimately generating greater emissions.

> The facts are clear: beyond a modest level, economic growth doesn't contribute at all to better health, longer life expectancy, falling indices of deprivation, or other metrics of a good life. In fact, in high GDP economies, further growth actually deepens inequality. For example, sharing resources effectively is an easy way to foster equality and use resources more efficiently, but sharing is antithetical to the logic of growth.

PH: Growth hates sharing. Every time you cook a meal for a friend or borrow a book from a library you damage GDP a tiny bit, because something that could have been traded has been given freely. Something patently resource efficient is diametrically opposed to our economic system.

MS: Continued dependence on this toxic system that drives colonial conquest, inequality, and climate breakdown is a choice. Better alternatives exist. Demand instead an economy whose goal isn't arbitrary, impossible, infinite extraction and expansion, but to ensure the health, happiness, and well-being of all.

PH: Demand an architecture that embraces sharing—vast libraries from which citizens can freely borrow any object for all manner of projects, from baby clothes to power tools to ballroom dresses to works of art.

23   **MS:**   Demand a fairer, more equal society, with an architecture and environment based on reciprocal care and repair, not neglect and ecological disaster.

PH: Demand the end of an economy of too much for too few and too little for too many.

MS: Demand an economy of plenty for all.

PH: Demand an end to endless growth.

MS: Enough!

The text first appeared in *Non-Extractive Architecture Vol. 1: On Designing Without Depletion* (Editor: Space Caviar, published by V-A-C Foundation, Moscow/Sternberg Press, London, 2021).

Kerem Halbrecht, Zachi Razel, Futures Probes, Nat Skoczylas, Eitan Nir, and Sarah Schalk

Non Voyage

On the Futures of Tourism Infrastructures

The Tourist Dilemma—A Tragicomedy

Deserted Planes

Touristoholics Anonymous

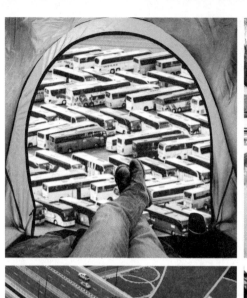

The Infrastructure of Desire

OFF SEASONS
Hotels and Resorts

33 Restrictions on travel prompted by the pandemic have crippled tourist infrastructures worldwide. At the same time, both suppliers and consumers of tourism experienced an intensified longing for regeneration. And that's something shared by the members of Non Voyage—a think-and-do-tank speculating about the potential of tourism infrastructures to become resources for planetary healing. In a kind of self-therapy, the members of the collective embark to find possible futures for decommissioned airplanes and closed hotels, for cities, regions, and landscapes. Transforming an airplane graveyard into a vacation resort, they create a site capable of fulfilling a broad variety of desires for vacation, reminiscent of experiments such as Biosphere 2 or simulated life on Mars. One finds here a comic strip recounting a group therapy session for tourism addicts who embody popular mass-tourism destinations. Or an advertisement for a hybrid hotel that makes use of its off-season to regenerate not only guests, but also landscapes, traditions, local economies, and the people who work in tourism. Or a series of images looking at the construction of the desires to travel and hacking them to ask questions about alternative desired objects and desiring subjects. Or an homage to the work Wheatfield by feminist land art artist Agnes Dennes, with links to the shipwreck of the Costa Concordia and the thirty-two lives it took, in a grounding caused by hubris and an unwillingness to take responsibility. In this cinematic image, Non Voyage offers an absurd perspective on the current moment of systemic tragedy, confronting us all, whether on voyage or not.

Image credits: All images by Non Voyage. Page 24: Image sources: dvoevnore, MehmetO, Shutterstock.com. Page 26: Illustration: Zachi Razel, Image sources: Aero Icarus. Page 28: Illustration: Katrina Guenther. Page 30: Image sources: Napoleon Sarony, Timo VolzHugo Veldtman, Mark Sisson, Simon Migaj, Ena Marinkovic, Aero Icarus, Denis Belitsky, Shutterstock.com, Shaiith, Adam Wasilewski, Abigail Marie, M-Production, Dana Cetojevic, Quark Studio, Jonathan Borba. Page 32: Olena Yakobchuk, Andrew Popov, Lukman Kakim, Shutterstock.com.

Felix Hartenstein

The No- Retail City

New Concepts for City Centers

"I'm going into town today" is a phrase often heard in German households—"Ich gehe heute in die Stadt." It is synonymous with going shopping and running errands. But behind the pragmatic pretext lies another, more subtle layer. Going into town, into a city, also means strolling and drifting, meeting other people, seeing and hearing "what's going on," feeling the pulse of a city, feeling that one belongs to the urban community. More than eighty years ago, Lewis Mumford, an early pioneer of urban thought, replied to the question posed in his now famous essay "What is a City?" by calling it a "theater of social action."[1] As Mumford writes: "The city fosters art and is art; the city creates the theater and is the theater." And it is this "social drama," he argues, that makes the city as such, distinguishing it from the countryside: "The city creates drama; the suburb lacks it." Jane Jacobs, perhaps the best known of all urban critics, similarly uses the metaphor of a stage in The Death and Life of Great American Cities, illustrating the public life of the city as a "sidewalk ballet."[2]

1   Lewis Mumford, "What is a City?" (1937) in The City Reader, ed. Richard T. LeGates and Frederic Stout, 5th edition (London: Routledge, 2011): 91–95.
2   Jane Jacobs, The Death and Life of Great American Cities (New York: Vintage Books, 1961): 50–54.

What would it ideally look like—this kind of a city backdrop creating such a wonderful stage for social interaction? Few people would imagine one of the monotonous shopping streets that dominate many city centers with the same chain stores. The imagination rather paints a picture of a neighborhood that has developed over time, with many small, very different stores lined up next to each other. And between them: doctors' offices, the post office, a bank, maybe a movie theater. Many of us will still remember such downtowns, looking back nostalgically. What has become of them? We know the story well, and it has played out in many places in a similar way. First came the supermarkets: large stores on the outskirts of a town or in industrial parks, accessible only by car. Shopping malls soon followed, brownfield developments away from the city. Once urban planners realized these developments were drawing purchasing power and foot traffic away from core areas, many municipalities were eager to lure them to the city center as alleged salvation. Today, almost every midsized city has its own shopping center. But the accompanying strengthening of urban centers that was promised unanimously has materialized in only a few places.

Disruptive Online Trade

Since the emergence of online retail, all areas of brick-and-mortar retail have been facing major challenges. Internet retailers are increasing their market share every year, and physical shopping in stores increasingly appears to be a thing of the past. As a result of the rapid changes that have shaped commerce in recent decades, urban planners are seeing a worrying trend: more and more stores are closing, and city centers are in danger of becoming deserted. The drop in retail sales that has come from the pandemic, along with the simultaneous push for online retail, are reinforcing this trend. There is currently nothing to suggest it will ever reverse. For many centuries, cities were also centers of trade. This era could now be coming to an end.[3] Several branches of trade with significance for daily needs have already largely disappeared from city centers: classic crafts that directly sell their wares, such as bakeries and butchers; as well as bookstores, music stores, shoe stores, and stationery shops. Many bank and post office branches

3   See Peter Laudenbach, "Was kommt nach der Einkaufsstraße?," *brand eins*, November 2020, 58–63.

have also been closed. Pharmacies are a rare exception. Thanks to legal privileges and clever lobbying, they have so far been able to hold their own against mail-order competition.

The Pandemic's Winners and Losers

The COVID-19 pandemic is adding to the pressure on retailers and accelerating existing trends. Although sales in the stationary retail sector rose by 3.9 percent overall in 2020 according to the German Retail Association, the effects were very unevenly distributed.[4] The textile trade recorded particularly large drops in revenue. Because clothing stores had to remain closed for long periods, sales fell by 23 percent.[5] Online retail, by contrast, once again posted strong growth, with sales rising by 20.7 percent.[6] Traditional department stores, with their extensive product ranges, are directly competing with e-commerce and are being left behind. However, individual offline industries were also able to expand their business during the pandemic. Home improvement stores, bicycle stores, and furniture stores benefited from the change in buying behavior during the lockdown. Supermarkets registered increased spending on groceries as many people worked from home, reduced their social contacts, and traveled less. In general, chain stores and large retail groups can more easily compensate for the effects of pandemic-related restrictions than can owner-operated stores. These larger businesses have financial leeway and the necessary resources to respond flexibly to the dynamic situation, which allows them to try out new formats. Many specialist retailers and small stores, however, are suffering from the effects of the crisis in a way that threatens their existence. For them, the very survival of their business is at stake. This is why economic experts fear a wave of bankruptcies, which would render city centers even less attractive.

4   See Handelsverband Deutschland (HDE), "Einzelhandel erlebt 2020 Jahr der Extreme: Coronakrise bringt viele Händler an den Rand der Insolvenz," February 1, 2021, https://einzelhandel.de/presse/aktuellemeldungen/13150-einzelhandel-erlebt-2020-jahr-der-extreme-coronakrise-bringt-viele-haendler-an-den-rand-der-insolvenz, last accessed February 22, 2021.
5   Ibid.
6   Ibid.

The threat posed by the decline of retail to many city centers is widely known. In addition to trade associations, municipal associations as well as local, state, and federal politicians have long since recognized the urgency of the issue. The first, obvious reflex is usually to want to save the stores. One of the most frequently mentioned solutions is to digitize retail—a move also supported by the German Federal Ministry of Economics. In October 2020, a round-table on this topic was held under the title "Preventing the Death of Retail: Revitalizing City Centers." The bottom line: "Digitization and the creation of spaces for culture and gastronomy … are decisive factors for vibrant city centers."[7] Digitizing offerings, however, involves considerable effort on the part of retailers. First, the technical challenges must be overcome: an online presence needs to be created and maintained. In addition to the sales website and an online payment system, this usually includes social media channels that require intensive supervision.

Various providers, including many well-known tech companies, now offer services tailored to retailers. eBay, which used to be known primarily as an auction platform for used items, is itself more and more frequently offering new goods for sale. The platform is becoming increasingly attractive for commercial sellers, who can set up an online store with relatively little effort. Amazon is probably the largest and best-known marketplace for third-party sellers in Germany. External sellers can use Amazon's site to post and sell their own items. For a fee, Amazon also handles warehousing and shipping. However, Amazon has repeatedly been accused of putting small merchants at a disadvantage. In addition, conflicts of interest arise when retailers offer products that Amazon also sells in a similar form. Google is also intensively courting retailers and has launched an initiative called ZukunftHandel in cooperation with the German Retail Association. Sellers can participate in free training sessions and receive a guide for online business. With the help of Google's range of services, they can, among other things, create company profiles, make it easier to find their web pages online, optimize their web presence, and place targeted advertisements.

7   Federal Ministry for Economic Affairs and Energy (BMWi), "Altmaier: 'Innenstädte sollen wieder Lieblingsplätze werden,'" October 20, 2020, https://www.bmwi.de/Redaktion/ /DE/Pressemitteilungen/2020/10/20201020-altmaier-innenstaedte-sollen-wiederlieblingsplaetze-werden.html, last accessed February 22, 2021.

In order to counter the dominance of the large platforms and
provide local merchants with alternative avenues to digitization,
numerous municipalities have set up city- or region-wide merchant
platforms. Many of these platforms have been tried out, but none
have been able to truly establish themselves anywhere. One possible reason: customers like comfort. They prefer platforms where
they can browse through as many different products as possible.
But local merchant platforms usually only cover a very limited
range, and they suffer from having a low profile.

In addition to the technical equipment, it is mainly daily operations
that pose major challenges to the digitization of retail. Products
must be entered, described, and priced on the website. Shipping,
returns, and complaints must be managed. The logistical effort is
enormous and personnel-intensive. Small retailers often cannot
afford this—or they have to become dependent on the platforms
that dominate the market. The fear is thus justified that the digitization of brick-and-mortar retail will not work on a large scale.
The established platforms—eBay for second-hand goods, Etsy for
homemade items, Zalando for clothing, Otto for all kinds of things,
and Amazon for nearly everything—will always be more efficient at
doing online business than small retailers, who do not have comparable storage capacities, logistics structures, customer centers,
and IT departments at their disposal. Even the parcel levy currently
being discussed for online retailers will not be able to fundamentally change this. While such an instrument can contribute to better
tax equity and allow online retailers to share in the costs of the
municipal infrastructure they use, the general competitive disadvantage of brick-and-mortar retailing remains.

The Pandemic as a Boost for New Retail Concepts

Even before the COVID-19 pandemic, retail companies were experimenting with new sales concepts. For some, the crisis has been
an opportunity to make the leap to the mass market.

Click and Collect: This form of distribution received a significant
boost during lockdown. With click and collect, goods are ordered
online and picked up in or outside a store. If this trend continues,
the question arises as to whether branches in their current form
will still be needed at all in the long term. It is conceivable that in
the future retail chains will increasingly rely on what is called the

long-tail approach: all items will be available without the need to have them in stock on-site.[8]

genialokal: Order Online, Pick Up in Bookstore

The genialokal platform is based on the catalog and logistics of the intermediary bookseller Libri. Customers can order more than six million books online and pick them up at more than 700 owner-operated bookstores. The offer also includes e-books, audio books, and toys.

Retail as a Service: In this concept, sales areas are rented out for a certain period of time to changing manufacturers to present their products. The focus is on ambiance, advice, and product presentation. Items can be touched and tested, making up for the last notable competitive disadvantage of Internet retailing, namely the lack of haptic experience. Purchases can be made immediately in the store—where the goods can be paid for but often not taken away immediately—or later on the Internet. Amazon is also experimenting with these kinds of concepts: in pop-up stores and standalone bookstores, which are largely designed as exhibition spaces, Amazon is offering a rotating range of products and testing hybrid sales concepts.[9]

Hybrid Niche Models: To help them stand out from the competition, more and more retailers are choosing the path of radical specialization. Instead of offering a wide range of products, they are reducing their offering to a few selected sectors. They share this expertise not only in-store but also through various online channels, where they create significant value for their followers by highlighting their uniqueness. They are thus equally retailers and influencers.[10] Nevertheless, the risk remains that customers will take advantage of their advice while making a purchase elsewhere. This model is therefore particularly suitable for individual products that are not

8   See Stephan A. Jansen, "Wie geht Konsumgesellschaft ohne Konsum?," brand eins, November 2020, 44–50.

9   See Felix Hartenstein, "Amazon: Vom Buchhändler zum Städtebauer," Baunetzwoche vol. 546 (2019): 6–18.

10 See Jens Bergmann, "Der moderne Verkäufer ist Influencer: Interview mit Alexander Graf," brand eins, November 2020, 52–55.

From vacancy to stage: Surfing in the basement of the department store L&T in the German town of Osnabrück. Photo: dpa

interchangeable and therefore not available elsewhere.[11] Alternative earning opportunities also arise from advertising revenue on
social platforms and affiliate marketing: influencers place links to
an online store on their websites or in social media. If a purchase is
made through these links, the influencers share in the proceeds.

Der Held der Steine:
Trader and Influencer

Thomas Panke has been running a store for Lego and other
kinds of toy bricks in Frankfurt am Main since 2013. On his
YouTube channel "Held der Steine," or "Brick Hero," he presents Lego products and compatible suppliers. Using humor
and a wealth of knowledge, Panke has managed to build a
large fan and customer base. His videos each reach hundreds
of thousands of viewers: in 2020, they were viewed a total
of more than sixty million times. Given this high number of
clicks, it can be assumed that these videos now have a significant impact on Panke's revenue through upstream advertising and affiliate links. But it's worth asking to what extent
the urban environment also benefits from Panke's store and
whether its success can serve as a model for other retailers.
Some buyers travel a long way to purchase sets at Held
der Steine that they could also get at other stores or on the
Internet—often at lower prices. Still, the store, with a walk-in
sales area of only a few square meters, is open just three days
a month. At best, it is helping revitalize the surrounding area
only to a very limited extent.

Panke has earned a reputation as a specialist in the field of
plastic brick toys that sets him apart from his competitors.
Retailers in other product segments often have comparable
expertise, but building a strong fan base via YouTube or other
social media requires a great deal of ongoing effort. This
model is thus not entirely suitable for imitation.

11   See Juliane Ribbeck-Lampel, "Chancen der Digitalisierung für den stationären
      Einzelhandel: Kleinflächenkonzepte in Innenstädten und ländlichen Räumen,"
      ARL News, February 1, 2020, 72–75.

It is becoming clear that sales and floor space are increasingly being decoupled, and that retail is to a certain degree becoming less dependent on physical space (with the exception of logistics centers and omnipresent parcel services). But what does that leave for brick-and-mortar retail? And how are cities affected when shopping consists primarily of pickup? One possible answer lies in personal contact with the customer, i.e., in how they are approached and advised, as well as in downstream services such as complaints, repairs, and returns. Although some stores continue to exist, they are gradually being transformed into interchangeable service centers. One wonders if that's enough to keep city centers vibrant.

A Radical New Beginning: A Thought Experiment

What would become of urban centers if shopping, as a practical reason for going into town, were to be eliminated? Would the social aspects of a city center—the encounters and exchanges it fosters—also disappear? Or are there ways to turn city centers into attractive places for spending time together, even without stores, shopping streets, and malls? What if community experiences were no longer seen as positive side effects of shopping but became the main attraction? Could going into a city center or into town take on a new meaning? Could it help to build community? And how could design help shape this experience?

One way of dealing with the shrinking retail sector that has received little attention so far would be to simply let it die, rather than artificially keeping it alive through expensive rescue measures. Any subsidies saved could instead be invested in cities' sociospatial infrastructure, in places where the money could yield a high social added value. It is extremely unlikely that brick-and-mortar retail will actually die out completely in the future. It is nonetheless worth examining this intentionally drastic scenario in order to broaden the scope of discourse and to sketch out alternatives in the event that the current trend toward the emptying out of city centers continues.

So let's imagine a future—perhaps a not too distant future—in which most stores are closed and goods are mostly purchased online. What at first seems like a horror scenario opens up unexpected possibilities upon closer inspection. Especially in cities with a lot of vacancies, social innovations, and a strong focus on the common good could provide new impetus for urban development.[12] Even without retail, cities will remain important economic centers. The vacancies left behind will open up space for other kinds of business that previously had no opportunity to set up shop in urban cores because store rents were too high.

Handwerkerhof Ottensen: Trade is Heading Up

The Handwerkerhof Ottensen in Hamburg-Altona—a center for skilled craftspeople—exemplifies that urban production is also possible as mixed use, in a vertical arrangement and a central location. Glaziers, carpenters, and plumbers, as well as various offices and law firms, instrument-making work-shops, and a Shiatsu practice are spread across four floors.

Abandoned department stores offer ideal conditions for commer-cial mixed-use models. They were often built in the 1970s using concrete-based skeleton construction and therefore allow max-imum flexibility. They can be converted almost at will and enable modular concepts for an agile coexistence of production and crafts, offices (coworking), education and research, social facilities, community venues—and even housing. Instead of eking out their existence as artifacts of decline, these obsolete buildings could become new anchors for urban society.

12   "Zukunft der (Stadt-)Zentren ohne Handel? Neue Impulse und Nutzungen für Zentren mit Zukunft," Positionspapier 116 (Hannover: Akademie für Raumentwicklung in der Leibniz-Gemeinschaft [ARL], 2020).
13   See Wenzel Meyer, "Paradigmenwechsel: Transformation Kaufhaus Darmstadt," https://plattformnachwuchsarchitekten.de/pdf/stadt-im-wandel-stadt-der-ideen-2020-erster-preis-paradigmenwechsel-transformation-kaufhaus-berlin.pdf f, last accessed February 22, 2021.

Paradigm Shift:
Transformation of a Department Store in Darmstadt

A concept for the conversion of the Karstadt building in Darmstadt won first place in the Young Architects Platform competition.[13] The proposal follows the approach of "socially resocializing" monofunctional buildings. A partial demolition will create a new town square, and a roof garden will complement the public space. This program for creating new space "will realize a new point of attraction through a synergy of culture, consumption, and creativity."[14]

Vacant stores can also give new impetus to lifeless city centers through community-oriented reprogramming. What is known as the Kreuzberg mixture can serve as a model. This Berlin district is known for its heterogeneous ground floor uses. Since the 1980s, many social institutions have taken up residence in former stores and craft workshops. Together, they facilitate a lively public and strengthen the social cohesion of the neighborhood.

The concept of a 15-minute city takes a very similar approach. It imagines that all facilities for daily needs should be accessible within fifteen minutes—without a car. Workplaces, schools, daycare centers, medical facilities, public authorities, shopping facilities, cultural offerings, playgrounds, sports areas, and recreational areas—all in the immediate vicinity. The goal is compact cities with short distances and decentralized public services at the neighborhood level. Such cities are not only more livable but also more climate-friendly. Paris has already embarked on this path and is planning a large-scale redistribution of street space in favor of public spaces for residents.[15] Comparable approaches can also be

14   Ibid.
15   In 2020, Paris Mayor Anne Hidalgo was reelected after making the 15-minute city (*Ville du quart d'heure*) a campaign promise.

found in the New Leipzig Charter,[16] the guiding document for urban
policy in Germany and Europe.[17]

Urban development has become inconceivable without digitization. Whether it concerns retail, leisure, or entertainment: city centers are in competition with various online offerings. To survive in the face of these digital alternatives, they must be "better" than the Internet. They won't accomplish this by competing in areas that are more efficient, convenient, or cheaper to regulate online. Rather, cities need to highlight the qualities that the Internet does not offer. First and foremost, this includes human interaction—contacts that are face to face instead of screen to screen.

The COVID-19 pandemic has impressively demonstrated the possibilities and limitations of digital communication. While video conferencing and chat groups allow work teams, clubs, friends, and other groups to stay in touch, they cannot replace face-to-face meetings. After several months of lockdown and working from home, a noticeable Zoom fatigue has set in for many people.

People have a deep need for physical closeness, for touch and the experience of togetherness. A lack of these things can lead to lone-liness and depression. In this regard, the long-term effects of the pandemic cannot be predicted yet. However, there is growing evi-dence that isolation has negatively impacted psychological health for many people or exacerbated existing mental health conditions. What cities need most after the pandemic is thus spaces that allow people to live out their longing for encounter and exchange. Third places are predestined for this purpose. These can be cafés, hair salons, park benches, kiosks, snack bars, or sports fields. What they have in common is that they create a pleasant atmosphere in which casual conversations can take place, while remaining open to newcomers. Public spaces also need to be designed to provide

16   See Bundesministerium des Innern, für Bau und Heimat (BMI), "New Leipzig Charter: The Transformative Power of Cities for the Common Good," November 20, 2020, https://ec.europa.eu/regional_policy/en/information/publications/brochures/2020/new-leipzig-charter-the-transformative-power-of-cities-for-the-common-good, last accessed February 22, 2021.
17   The New Leipzig Charter was adopted at the Informal Ministerial Meeting on Urban Development during Germany's 2020 EU Council Presidency. It states: "Transforming central urban areas into attractive multifunctional spaces provides new opportunities for urban development through mixed use for living, working, and recreation, where manufacturing, retail, and services are found alongside housing, hospitality, and leisure." New Leipzig Charter, 5.

space for community experiences and recreation—ideally in combination with significant green space and noncommercial offerings that function as true social spaces.[18]

New Life in Empty Stores

A decisive factor for the future of cities lies in access to real estate and its uses. Real-estate owners often leave storefronts vacant for long periods of time. They are speculating on a recovery of the market and hoping for higher rental income in the long term, rather than opening the space to other uses in the short term. However, if a store cannot be rented out at conditions acceptable to the owner over a longer period of time, economic pressure increases—and with it the willingness to think about alternative concepts and consider suggestions from others.

Local authorities have a key role to play here. They can serve as intermediaries between commercial property owners and new user groups. They can also make owners aware of the external social costs of vacancy and offer support in testing unconventional measures to revitalize vacant properties.

The transformation of city centers requires new alliances and models for business, both in the private sector and in municipal policy, that increasingly focus on the common good of urban areas. In this way, buildings or city districts can be viewed as a holistic system, allowing positive synergies to be more effectively utilized. For example, formats such as coworking and Production 4.0 on upper floors can lead to new revenue opportunities that offset potential revenue shortfalls on the first floor. Similarly, high-frequency but low-revenue uses can be subsidized by a neighborhood if it benefits from their presence. In this way, a "center yield" could be generated in addition to real-estate profit. But to meet these requirements, municipalities need suitable procedures and instruments. State and federal policymakers are called upon to

---

18   The New Leipzig Charter accordingly notes: "Services and infrastructure for the common good" include "health care, social services, education, cultural services, housing, water and energy supply, waste management, public transport, digital networks and information systems. Furthermore, the quality of public spaces including green and blue infrastructure as well as the preservation and revitalisation of built cultural heritage are important." New Leipzig Charter, 6.

provide the appropriate funding instruments to realize these goals.
Further assistance would be provided by extending or facilitating
the municipal right of first refusal for commercial real estate.

From Vacancy to Stage

Now as then, a livable city is too often thought of in terms of retail.
The prevailing belief is that appealing shopping options attract
residents to the center and draw visitors from the surrounding area.
This higher purchasing power supposedly allows the local economy
to flourish; and quite incidentally, this assumption continues, lively
streets and squares are created. But this calculation is working
out less and less frequently. Monofunctional city centers have
long since lost their appeal—especially when the design of public
spaces is primarily adapted to the requirements of retail functions
and social aspects play a subordinate role at best. The desolation
of such one-sided city centers becomes apparent at the latest after
closing time.

What remains, however, are the social needs of the people.
Responses to pandemic-related restrictions have further
highlighted this fact. It is likely that in the aftermath of the pandemic, many people will have a strong desire to meet and share
experiences.

The German Federal Economics Minister Peter Altmaier said at the
roundtable on the future of city centers: "City centers once again
need to become places where people love to be."[19] One can only
agree. But these favorite places could, indeed must, look different
from what we currently see. The future of livable cities lies not in
saving retail but in creating offerings that once again focus on the
social and cultural qualities of city centers: more stage, less staging.

19 Bundesministerium für Wirtschaft und Energie, "Altmaier: 'Innenstädte sollen wieder Lieblingsplätze werden.'"

Urban Ob-solescences

Future Fields of Urban Transformation, Made Visible by the Pandemic

In 1956, Malcom McLean, a shipowner specializing in freight forwarding, deployed containers to transport goods for the first time, utilizing a tanker specially converted for this purpose, the Ideal X. His invention not only revolutionized global logistics but also had disruptive effects on how ports were being used. Many port facilities in European cities were no longer capable of handling these steadily growing container ships; they were therefore either or completely abandoned or relocated. Such obsolescences in cities—which is to say functions that have fallen into disuse but harbor great potential—are not new. There are numerous further examples, such as the closing down of military barracks after the fall of the Berlin Wall, old industrial areas that became obsolete in the course of globalization, or centrally located freight yards that have been replaced by freight villages on the edges of cities. Other formerly urban features such as slaughterhouses, breweries, or wholesale markets have likewise been relocated to points of high accessibility, as they are often called, because these locations are integrated into international or at least transregional production and supply chains.

In sum, these have been enormous and, more importantly, valuable spaces for developing interior urban areas. They are usually centrally located, well developed, and relatively easy to reconfigure since the property is either publicly owned or belongs to a single industrial owner. Such spatial resources have provided the foundations for attractive developments like the HafenCity in Hamburg,

the Überseestadt in Bremen, the Ackermannbogen in Munich,
or creative districts such as the Baumwollspinnerei in Leipzig.
Moreover, these areas have been badly needed. Since the 1990s,
major cities as well as smaller university towns (known in German
as "Schwarmstädte," or boomtowns attracting many new residents)
have grown rapidly, and the discussion around housing shortages
and rising rents has not stopped. A megatrend is operating here in
the background: both knowledge culture and a knowledge-based
society are driving a structural transformation of the job market.
And it is precisely in big cities and university towns that creative
industries are concentrated, along with major centers of research
and development with attractive, good-paying jobs.

Megatrends and the Transformations of Tomorrow

Fundamental social developments, known as megatrends, thus
directly affect the way space is utilized, triggering both shortages
of space as well as vacancies with potential for new uses. From
this perspective, the urban obsolescences of the last decades
were a byproduct of globalization and its logistics. The apparent
singular effect of the container must also be viewed in this context.
Similar concepts had already been developed in 1933 by the Bureau
Internationale des Containers (BIC) in Paris, but they were initially
scrapped due to cost-benefit considerations.[1] Still, it was only a
matter of time before this niche innovation led to fundamental
changes in the transportation of goods.

Can we use these experiences from the past to ascertain which
areas of the city will become obsolete in the future and which types
of buildings will be impacted? On the one hand, this can be done
by methodically investigating the effects that megatrends have on
space and how they interact and mutually reinforce each other. In
all likelihood the future fields of transformation will no longer tend
to extensive and large-scale, as before, but will rather be scaled
into smaller units and more dispersed. And on the other hand,
it is already becoming clear that other megatrends, especially
digitalization, will affect spatial and architectural typologies in ways
that differ from the past. Overlapping dynamics are also evolving,
for instance climate change and transformations in energy and

1   See Johanna Lutteroth, "Container-Revolution: Welterfolg mit der Wunderkiste,"
     Der Spiegel, July 7, 2011, https://www.spiegel.de/geschichte/container-revolution-
     welterfolg-mit-der-wunderkiste-a-947252.html, last accessed March 7, 2021.

transport, that will impact the use of areas devoted to transit and the architecture of mobility.

In the future, the spaces that will be affected are those belonging to the categories of commerce, work, mobility, culture, and religion, that is, those occupying a clearly defined position within urban agglomerations. Location will be the decisive factor, as not every site faces a risk, or one that is equally high, that its urban function will become obsolete. Due to the acute scarcity of space in cities, it seems that predictively identifying and systematically tapping those resources will be a fundamental task of urban development.

Digitalization and Space

Currently it is becoming extremely apparent just how strongly digitalization is impacting almost all spheres of life and thus also the transformation of work and commerce. COVID-19 is operating here only as a catalyst, not a trigger. Brick-and-mortar shops have long been under pressure from the platform economy represented by Amazon and the like, and in the cultural arena streaming services have been battering movie theaters for quite some time. The pandemic has generated further disruption such that analog actors are being forced to stand by and watch, defenseless, as their business models crumble.

In the office-space and service sectors, businesses offering software for videoconferencing are calling the classical office tower into question. To be sure, the field of planning erred in the 1990s in predicting that the emergence of the Internet and the possibility of telecommuting would mean that urban sprawl would ultimately prevail as the dominant form of settlement, but at that time digitalization was still in its infancy. There were no professional video client applications and no 5G technology. According to a survey by the General German Automobile Association (ADAC), the number of daily commuters declined 18 percent during the second lockdown in the winter of 2020, even dropping a full 34 percent during the very first lockdown in the spring.[2] Meanwhile, large companies have already calculated how much savings they can achieve through remote work, both in terms of space and overhead costs.

2   See ADAC, "Corona und Mobilität" Mehr Homeoffice, weniger Berufsverkehr," November 24, 2020, https://www.adac.de/verkehr/standpunkte-studien/mobilitaets-trends/corona-mobilitaet/, last accessed March 7, 2021.

Megatrends and urban typologies, source: N. Beucker, S. Rettich, S. Tastel—research group
"Obsolete Stadt," 2020

52

TYPOLOGIES OF OBSOLESCENCE

MEGATRENDS

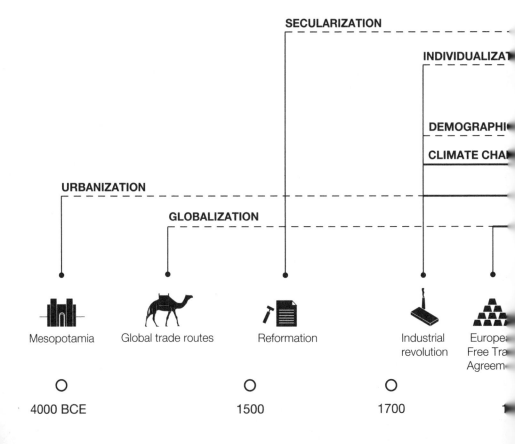

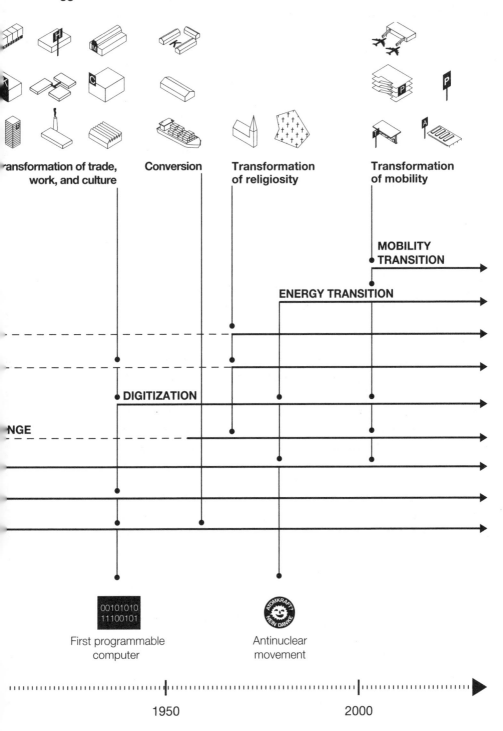

ansformation of trade, work, and culture

Conversion

Transformation of religiosity

Transformation of mobility

MOBILITY TRANSITION

ENERGY TRANSITION

DIGITIZATION

NGE

First programmable computer

Antinuclear movement

1950

2000

Downtown areas, which are predominantly characterized by stationary retail and office spaces, are thus being particularly impacted
by the pandemic and the spatial ramifications of digitalization. If, for
example, one observes the retail sector from a multilevel perspective that distinguishes among megatrends (landscape-level), stakeholders (regime-level), and innovations (niche-level), it becomes
apparent how these levels are interconnected in ways that not only
establish disruptions but also allow for transformations to develop.
At the same time, the crisis of city centers is opening up a window
of opportunity. Typologies that have become obsolete are offering
space for things like residential living. The former department store,
for instance, lends itself to social or cultural uses and could be
developed into the heart of a district though a horizontal functional
structure. Such diverse, mixed-use spaces boost the resilience of
central urban cores.

Processes of digitalization have also precipitated a realignment
in the production sector. The growing use of information technology and robotics is leading here to a surplus of space. Due to
demographic changes that will mitigate job loss, no great upheaval
is anticipated for the job market. Overall, however, considerable
displacements from the production sector into the areas of
information technology and services are expected.[3] Specifically
for Industry 4.0, as it is called, fewer skilled trade workers will
be needed, but more computer scientists. Single-story factory
buildings could give way to software companies that are organized
vertically, while at the same time providing new spaces for apartments. The influence this will have on the job market and thus on
the need for space depends on the industry and even varies considerably among different segments of manufacturing. Using the
example of Volkswagen in the automobile industry, it is estimated
that by 2029 the transition to electric mobility in car manufacturing
will only result in a roughly 12 percent decline in employment. The
situation for the manufacturing of component parts, in particular
for external suppliers, looks rather more dire: here it is expected
that up to 70 percent fewer jobs will be required since the electric
engine involves considerably fewer individual parts and manufacturing steps.[4]

3   See Institut für Arbeitsmarkt- und Berufsforschung, "Industrie 4.0 und die Folgen
     für Arbeitsmarkt und Wirtschaft," Bericht 16 (2015), http://doku.iab.de/aktuell/2015/
     aktueller_bericht_1516.pdf, last accessed March 7, 2021: 1.

In addition to digitalization, it is climate change and the connected transformations in energy and mobility, as well as changes in the role and practice of religion in society, that will constitute the future megatrends impacting the functioning and development of cities and their spaces. Even if cars regain some of their importance in the pandemic, climate change will in the long run make a transition to sustainable forms of energy and transport inevitable. Pop-up bike lanes are a kind of harbinger of this development. Reclaiming space will be an important goal given reduced traffic, since far fewer parking spaces and garages will be needed. The question is only when and whether further disruptive events, such as the Volkswagen emissions scandal, will be necessary for comprehensive political action to be taken. The gains in available space would be immense: in a city like Hamburg, there are currently more than 700 hectares of surface area devoted solely to parking.[5] Calculations show that depending on the local circumstances one car-sharing vehicle replaces four, and in some cases up to ten private ones.[6] Assuming all car traffic were to be shifted to sharing services, in an ideal scenario 90 percent of parking spots could be eliminated. The actual level of reduction will settle somewhere in between, in accordance with daily mobility habits.

Even before the pandemic, some parking garage management companies such as APCOA Parking Germany had begun to rethink their business model. They want to overcome the negative image of gray and drafty garages and reshape these sites as urban hubs, which is to say intermodal transfer points for various forms of transport. Even the lobbying group Bundesverband Parken (German Parking Association) speaks of a paradigm shift, envisioning other functions like cafés or bike-lending and repair stations on the ground floors of converted parking garages, such as

4   See Fraunhofer IAO, Wilhelm Bauer, Oliver Riedel, and Florian Herrmann, eds., "Beschäftigung 2030—Auswirkungen von Elektromobilität und Digitalisierung auf die Qualität und Quantität der Beschäftigung bei Volkswagen, Kurzfassung," https://www.iao.fraunhofer.de/content/dam/iao/images/iao-news/beschaeftigung-2030-kurzfassung.pdf, last accessed March 7, 2021: 2.

5   Stefan Rettich and Sabine Tastel, unpublished estimate, research group "Obsolete Stadt," 2021.

6   See Umweltbundesamt, "CarSharing nutzen," April 10, 2021, https://www.umweltbundesamt.de/umwelttipps-fuer-den-alltag/mobilitaet/carsharing-nutzen#unsere-tipps, last accessed April 10, 2021.

	RETAIL					CULTURE	WORK		
(I)	+		+	+		+			−
(II)	+	+			+	+	+	+	−
(III)	+	+					+	+	−
(IV)		+	+		+	+	+	+	−

LEGEND

(I) Center
(II) Inner-City
(III) Outer-City
(IV) Agglomeration

 Owner-run retail

 Large-scale retail

 Shopping mall

 Department store

	TRANSPORTATION					RELIGION		CONVERSION		
		Gas station	Parking garage	Parking lot	Airport	Cemetery	Church	Barracks	Late 19th-century factory	Port logistics
			+				+			
+	+	+	+			+	+		+	+
	+	+	+			+	+	+		+
	+	+	+	+						

ide fair		Office building		Parking lot		Barracks		
ovie theater		Car dealership		Airport		Late 19th-century factory		
anufacturing		Gas station		Cemetery		Port logistics		
ustry		Parking garage		Church				

the one currently planned by E. Breuninger GmbH & Co.[7] Its garage
in downtown Stuttgart is to be redeveloped as a smart mobility hub
with a bustling ground floor, and to provide space for the Haus für
Film und Medien.[8] During the pandemic approximately 50 percent
of short-term parkers in the downtown areas disappeared, and this
will undoubtedly accelerate the development toward the opening
up of parking garages for other functions. After all, in light of the
continued atrophy of the retail sector, more profit can be generated
with central coworking spaces or rooftop penthouses than with
empty parking places.

The Transformation of Religiosity

Secularization is a megatrend reaching especially far back in
history that has come to be discussed as a transformation of religiosity; as a topic, it is especially present in public consciousness
because an increased number of people are leaving the church.
The cases of abuse in the Catholic Church are having an additional
disruptive effect. In a study published in 2019, the Research Center
for Generational Contracts (FZG) projected a 49 percent drop in
members of the Evangelical and Catholic Churches in Germany by
2060; this projection was based not only on demographic changes
but also on general sociocultural developments such as the decline
in baptisms or these defections from the church.[9] In order to be
able to afford the "same basket of religious goods,"[10] churches
in 2060 will require approximately double the capital. And it has
already been seven years since the state initiative StadtBauKultur
NRW (StateBuildingCulture North Rhine-Westphalia) published
a 2014 study on the theme "Kirchen geben Raum: Empfehlungen
zur Neunutzung von Kirchengebäuden" (Churches Provide Space:
Recommendations for New Uses of Church Buildings). One of the
reasons for this publication was the public announcement by the

7   See Thomas Maier, "Was nach Corona aus den Parkhäusern wird," *FAZ*, January 4, 2021,
    https://www.faz.net/aktuell/rhein-main/frankfurt/autos-nach-corona-was-aus-dem-
    parken-in-staedten-wird-17128662.html, last accessed March 7, 2021.
8   See Konstantin Schwarz, "Breuninger-Garage: Jury kürt Sieger," *Stuttgarter
    Nachrichten*, December 20, 2020, https://www.stuttgarter-nachrichten.de/inhalt.
    wettbewerb-in-stuttgart-breuninger-garage-jury-kuert-sieger.b318dca0-a460-435f-
    a1da-5005703e81ca.html, last accessed March 7, 2021.
9   See Evangelische Kirche in Deutschland, "Langfristige Projektion der
    Kirchenmitglieder und des Kirchensteueraufkommens in Deutschland: Eine Studie des
    Forschungszentrums Generationsverträge an der Albert-Ludwig-Universität Freiburg,"
    (2019), https://www.ekd.de/ekd_de/ds_doc/projektion-2060-ekd-vdd-factsheet-2019.
    pdf, last accessed March 7, 2021: 8.
10 Ibid., 14

Ruhr diocese in 2005 that it would have to part with nearly 100 of the 350 churches it oversaw at the time.[11] The topic is a difficult one, since churches, both as institutions and as buildings, are accorded high social significance. The same holds true for the accompanying rectories and parish halls. Such sensitive properties also harbor great potential, as they are generally centrally located within neighborhoods and firmly anchored in the collective consciousness of local residents. They could thus also be put into service for other sociocultural uses in the area. By now one can find a series of excellent models for the conversion of churches, from the daycare center in the former St. Sebastian parish church in Münster to the König art gallery in the brutalist St. Agnes church in Berlin or a bookstore in what used to be the Dominican church in Maastricht.

Another significant phenomenon, the transformation of burial culture, is showing up in the demand for cemetery space. More than a third of this space in Germany is surplus. These spaces are no longer actively used, yet they must still be maintained at great expense, which places those managing the cemeteries under significant financial pressure.[12] This is because cemeteries in Germany are designed for the burial of coffins while the trend is toward urns; in Berlin, for example, this means that only a fourth of the available space is needed. Large sections of cemeteries could therefore be converted, after a respectful period of time, into areas for leisure and recreation.[13]

Several municipalities have already begun to establish plans for developing cemeteries in order to anticipate current and future usage requirements. One example is in Hamburg-Ohlsdorf, where 270 of the 400 hectares of the largest park cemetery in the world are designated for both intensive and extensive future use as a park.[14] Hamburg had a precedent in Wohlers Park for such repurposing. Since 1979, the 4.6-hectare area of the former Norderreihe cemetery in the district of Altona has been used in this way. The encircling wall, entrances, and pathways as well as the gravestones and monuments all give clear indications of the site's previous

11   See Jörg Best, "Kirchen geben Raum: Empfehlungen zur Neunutzung von Kirchengebäuden," (Gelsenkirchen: Landesinitiative StadtBauKultur NRW, 2020): 7 and 9.

12   See IKH – Institut für Kommunale Haushaltswirtschaft, "Wirtschaftlichkeit im Friedhofswesen," (Helsa, 2015): 23–24.

13   See Stefan Rettich, "Berlin denkt weiter," *Garten + Landschaft*, vol. 5 (2017): 42–45, here 42.

14   Freie und Hansestadt Hamburg, "Ohlsdorf 2050: Dokumentation des Beteiligungsprozesses" (Hamburg, 2016): 15.

Multilevel-perspective retail: the crisis opens a window of opportunity for niche innovation,
source: C. Brück, M. Gantert, S. Rettich, S. Tastel—research group "Obsolete Stadt," 2020

60

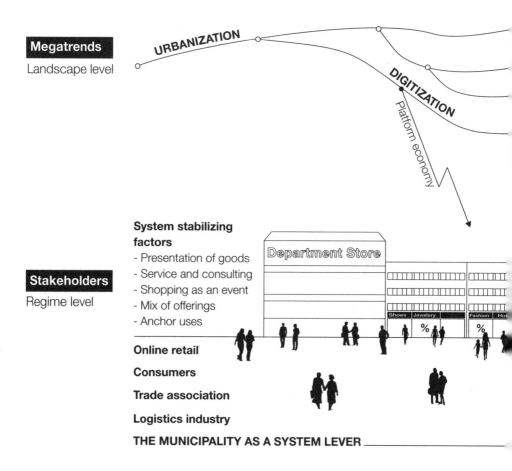

URBANIZATION

DIGITIZATION

Platform economy

System stabilizing factors
- Presentation of goods
- Service and consulting
- Shopping as an event
- Mix of offerings
- Anchor uses

Stakeholders

Regime level

Department Store

Shoes | Jewelry | Fashion | Ho

Online retail

Consumers

Trade association

Logistics industry

THE MUNICIPALITY AS A SYSTEM LEVER

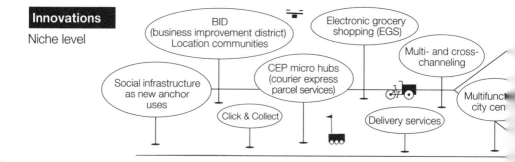

Innovations

Niche level

BID
(business improvement district)
Location communities

Electronic grocery
shopping (EGS)

Multi- and cross-
channeling

Social infrastructure
as new anchor
uses

CEP micro hubs
(courier express
parcel services)

Multifunct
city cen

Click & Collect

Delivery services

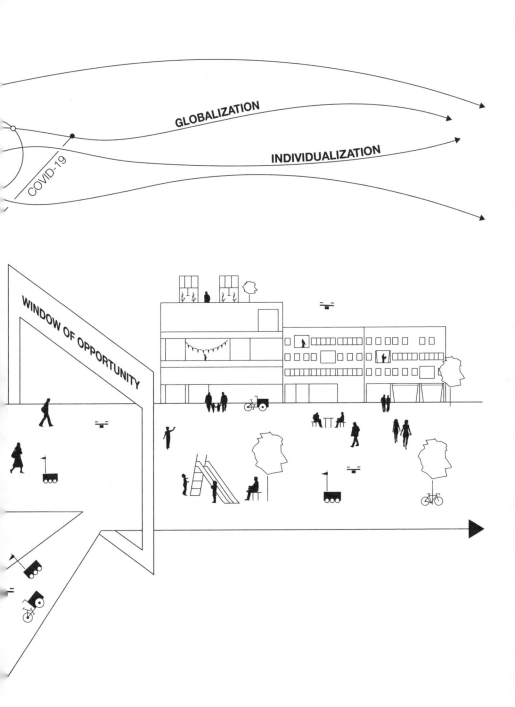

use; its contemplative atmosphere has prompted locals to call it "Tai-Chi Park" or "Meditation Park." In one particular case in Berlin-Neukölln, apartments and social facilities are even being built on unused parts of a former cemetery.

Churches could expand their charitable endeavors by utilizing space that is no longer needed, thereby tapping new audiences. The transformation in religiosity does not in itself mean that people are turning away from faith. The difference lies only in how that faith is practiced, and Christian ethics can perhaps be conveyed even more successfully through integrative residential models than with a sermon in a church.

COVID-19 and the Necessity of Redundancies

Cities are societies' vehicles of transformation. The New Leipzig Charter invokes this transformative power and its significance for the common good.[15] If there is one thing we can learn from the current crisis, it is that—against our better judgment—we have failed to address obvious areas of transformation. The call for resilience and resistance is therefore understandable, except that if the armoring that comes with such a stance were to be transferred to all members of the city it would undoubtedly weigh too heavily on everyday life. It would also hinder transformations where they are urgently needed, such as in our city centers; or it would support false path dependencies, for example on the car-friendly city, which is once again proving to be particularly resilient in the pandemic. Resilience is thus a double-edged sword: it supports both what is relevant and what is outdated.

Something else that is both relevant and in need of protection, however, is the neighborhood. Stay home, stay safe—the golden rule of the pandemic—underlines the importance of the home as a refuge, and that of neighborhoods in their social, spatial, and economic dimensions. This also aligns with current concepts such as

---

15   The New Leipzig Charter is a declaration by the ministers responsible for urban development in the European member states, which defined common cornerstones for urban development oriented towards the common good. It was signed in Leipzig on November 30, 2020. See BMI, "New Leipzig Charter: The Transformative Power of Cities for the Common Good," https://www.bmi.bund.de/SharedDocs/downloads/DE/veroeffentlichungen/2020/eu-rp/gemeinsame-erklaerungen/neue-leipzig-charta-2020.pdf;jsessionid=E82409E4CE128AC2AB2F45DECEA5A91D.1_cid295?__blob=publicationFile&v=6, last accessed March 7, 2021.

63 the 15-minute city.[16] If we look back into history, though, we see that almost all of these demands are already found in Jane Jacobs's four points on the diversity of cities.[17] So before discussing new guiding principles, it would make sense to first implement those that already exist, as they are obviously still valid today, and to advance pent-up transformations.

The crisis is also teaching us that the goals of sustainability can only be achieved through the use of substrategies. In addition to targeted resilience and subsistence, these are primarily redundancies—in global supply chains, in warehousing, or in those employed by municipalities and the health system. In urban development, too, we urgently need a stockpile that will once again give us space to deal with the "known unknowns," i.e., those challenges that we know about even if we do not know when and to what extent they will reappear on the scene.[18] And this applies not only to the current pandemic, but just as much to the global financial market crisis with its unexpected effects on land prices, real-estate prices, and rents; to migration movements with the spaces they require to house new arrivals; to the continuing influx into major cities and the associated housing shortage; and last but not least to climate change, which will bring many unexpected things for the future. We are aware of all of those challenges, and each one requires land for developing inner urban areas, which is scarce.

This is precisely why it is important to see the obsolescences of perspectives in cities as an opportunity—and not to leave these areas to the free play of the markets and speculation. The areas are needed more than ever, for urban development that is oriented toward the common good and that is climate-friendly.

The text is based on findings of the research project "Obsolete Stadt," which is funded by the Robert Bosch Foundation (www.obsolete-stadt.de).

16 See Carlos Moreno and Marina Garnier, "La Ville du quart heure," *Livre Blanc,* no. 2, https://www.dak.de/dak/download/forsa-umfrage-ergebnisse-2401560.pdf, last accessed April 4, 2021.

17 See Jane Jacobs, *The Death and Life of Great American Cities* (New York: Vintage Books, 1961), especially chapter 8–11, "The Need for Primary Mixed Uses," 152–177.

18 The term comes from Donald Rumsfeld and his paraphrasing of the issues facing the Third Gulf War. It has since come to be used by researchers in the field of risk assessments. See also Herfried Münkler and Marina Münkler, "Der Einbruch des Unvorhersehbaren und wie wir uns zukünftig darauf vorbereiten sollten," in *Jenseits von Corona: Unsere Welt nach der Pandemie—Perspektiven aus der Wissenschaft*, ed. Bernd Kortmann and Günther G. Schulze (Bielefeld: transcript Verlag, 2020): 103.

Un-spectacular

Small and Medium-Sized Cities Are Making an Impact on Urban Research

For a long time, urban research and city planning did not focus on small and medium-sized cities.[1] This was due in part to the fact that these places stood in the shadow of growing metropolitan areas and function in ways that are simple and unspectacular. It was not until the 2010s that the focus of politics and planning increasingly turned toward smaller cities through such programs as the state urban development fund Smaller Cities and Communities. This turn was also motivated by the fact that spatial disparities were increasing and becoming ever more visible between the prospering metropolitan regions profiting from reurbanization and the rural areas being left behind economically. Demographic changes have resulted in these places losing not only population and jobs, but also a part of their function.[2]

In the meantime, the future prospects of small and medium-sized cities have again become themes in debates among planners (and in the media), boosted by the increasing influx of young adults who have discovered life in the country in response to pressure from rising real-estate prices and rents in major cities, among other things. Current discussions around the significance of working

1   See Lars Porsche and Antonia Milbert, "Kleinstädte in Deutschland: Ein Überblick," *Informationen zur Raumentwicklung* (IzR) 6 (2018): 4–21.
2   See Bundesministerium des Innern, für Bau und Heimat (BMI), "Schwerpunktthema Stadtumbau in Klein- und Mittelstädten und Schlussfolgerungen für das neue Programm 'Wachstum und nachhaltige Erneuerung': Bundestransferstelle Stadtumbau" (Berlin, 2020): 4–6.

from home, which has experienced a boom in the time of COVID-19 and the accelerated digitalization (more or less voluntary) in many spheres of life, are amplifying this trend.[3]

The designation "small and medium-sized cities" is often used for the kinds of cities and municipalities classified somewhere between metropolis and rural area; a unitary concept of what exactly is denoted by this category does not exist.[4] The spatial monitoring system of the German Federal Institute for Research on Building, Urban Affairs, and Spatial Development (BBSR) classifies small cities as those with between 5,000 and 20,000 residents and at least one core function, e.g., food provisioning, and medium-sized cities as those with between 20,000 and 100,000 residents and a middle-order function, e.g., medical specialists or secondary schools. According to such a classification scheme there are currently 2,100 small and 620 medium-sized cities in Germany, which are together home to around 58 percent of the total population.[5]

Small and medium-sized cities stabilize rural areas as important sites for living, working, and commerce as well as social gathering. In addition, they offer a serene and livable environment and relieve pressure on tight housing markets in major cities.[6] The prospects for development are nonetheless not uniform; they are determined by the location of the particular city, which is to say by their proximity to major metropolitan areas and the transport links to them.

Structurally and historically, their centers are hardly different from those of larger cities. They are traditionally a functional mix of commerce, trade, industry, and housing as well as the visible architectural triad of church, city hall, and town square. In many cities these structures work together with public spaces to establish a distinctive identity.[7] But they are increasingly losing their significance.

---

3   See Simon Book et al., "Wie wir arbeiten, leben, wohnen werden," *Der Spiegel* 37 (2020): 10–19.

4   Lars Porsche, Annett Steinführer, Martin Sondermann, ed., "Kleinstadtforschung in Deutschland: Stand, Perspektiven und Empfehlungen," *Arbeitsberichte der ARL* 28 (Hannover: Akademie, 2019).

5   German Federal Institute for Research on Building, Urban Affairs and Spatial Development (BBSR), *Laufende Stadtbeobachtung—Raumabgrenzungen: Stadt- und Gemeindetypen in Deutschland* (Bonn, n.d.), as of 2017, https://www.bbsr.bund.de/BBSR/DE/forschung/raumbeobachtung/downloads/downloadsReferenz2.html.

6   See Silke Weidner, "Provinzstädte als Anker im Raum," in *Der Land in Sicht: Ländliche Räume in Deutschland zwischen Prosperität und Peripherisierung*, ed. Christian Krajewski and Claus-Christian Wiegandt (Bonn: bpb, 2020): 152 ff.

7   See Sascha Anders, Stefan Kreutz, and Thomas Krüger, "Corona und die Folgen für die Innenstädte," *Der Raumentwicklung* (IzR) 4 (2020): 58–64.

The fading importance of city centers has been hastened by the 66

proliferation of cars, a phenomenon that goes hand in hand with unappealing public transport options, especially in small communities. Competing locations or major cities in the region are generally reachable quickly and comfortably by car, and thus the need to seek out the nearby town center is no longer present. The emissions and land use of vehicle traffic have both played a part in the way public space has lost its function as a site for communication and spending time.

Meeting places have, as a result, been shifted either into the private sphere, into digital spaces or retail parks located outside the urban center, or to the next largest city. Country inns, which were once social gathering places in small towns, are becoming increasingly scarce.[8] Furthermore, urban structures scaled in small units are not compatible with the current spatial requirements of the retail or manufacturing sectors. Many jobs are now to be found in decentralized office locations, industrial parks, or in the central business districts of the next largest cities.

With the support of public funds and various development programs, it has been possible to renovate buildings in many cities and transform public space.[9] Family and community centers have been built,[10] along with housing and health centers, and former shopping centers have been repurposed or libraries refurbished.[11] Still, it has been impossible to stop the structural transformation that is underway, and the challenges for small and midsized cities stemming from it are well-known.

8   Anna Sprockhoff, "Landgasthöfe: Bis zum letzten Bier," *Zeit Online*, April 16, 2018, https://www.zeit.de/gesellschaft/2018-04/landgasthoefe-sterben-niedersachsen-neuhaus-ueberland-d18.
9   One example, among others, is funding within the incentive programs for urban development "Aktive Stadt- und Ortsteilzentren" and "Kleinere Städte und Gemeinden."
10   See Bundesministerium für Umwelt, Naturschutz, Bau und Reaktorsicherheit (BMUB), "Zukunftsweisende Ansätze in kleineren Städten und Gemeinden: Strategien und Projekte aus dem Städtebauförderungsprogramm" (Berlin, 2018), and the interim program evaluation for "Kleinere Städte und Gemeinden—überörtliche Zusammenarbeit und Netzwerke," final report, in cooperation with EBP (Bonn, 2020).
11   See BBSR, "Zehn Jahre Aktive Stadt- und Ortsteilzentren: Vierter Statusbericht zum Zentrenprogramm der Städtebauförderung" (Berlin/Bonn, 2018).

Recently, a series of analyses, development policy programs, and studies have grappled with the structural weaknesses of small and medium-sized cities. Many focused on the revitalization of town centers. The Federal Foundation of Baukultur (BSBK), for example, formulates three recommendations for action: "Strengthen and enliven the heart of an area," "a village needs diversity," and "the overall image of a place should be reinforced through its buildings."[12] They point to the importance of developing and implementing innovative, varied, and tailor-made ideas in the town center, highlighting property owners, social initiatives, and business owners as key players and stakeholders.

Similar strategic approaches are also emphasized by the BBSR in its 2018 study "Urbane Kleinstädte."[13] In the face of a declining and aging population, they recommend cultivating the specific qualities of a place and enhancing the quality of life locally for longtime residents as well as newcomers. The great challenge they identify is the persistent relegation of new sites for industry and housing to the outskirts of the city, which leads to the town center losing its function and to the increasing emptiness of its buildings—what is often called the donut effect. This is connected with the demand to revitalize the city center, the heart of the area, and to bolster the retail options it offers. The strained financial situation of many local authorities is also noted as a concern that must be addressed by revitalization programs, since weak municipal finances make investment more difficult in essential health and social services, local public transport, and the modernization of the technical infrastructure for the technologies of the future.[14] This includes digitalization, energy supply, and sustainable mobility concepts, which in turn sustain regional economic strength and preserve local employment.

"Lage und Zukunft der Kleinstädte in Deutschland" (Situation and Future of Small Towns in Germany), a study that appeared in 2019, addresses several of these themes and complements them with (urban) planning approaches for creating vital, mixed-use urban cores.[15] The study names, among other things, having a municipal

12   Bundesstiftung Baukultur (BSBK), Baukulturbericht 17, *Stadt und Land* (Potsdam, 2016).
13   BBSR, "Urbane Kleinstädte" (Bonn, 2020).
14   See ibid., 14–31.
15   See BBSR, "Lage und Zukunft der Kleinstädte in Deutschland—Bestandsaufnahme zur Situation der Kleinstädte in zentralen Lagen" (Bonn, 2020).

office that manages and coordinates retail offerings (a "care-taker"), applying specific urban-planning legislation and incentive schemes, ensuring access to food, primary schools, and daycare centers, and promoting cultural life. In addition, the study highlights both new housing construction and the development of existing stock as well fostering trade and industry.[16]

Parallel to these rather traditional studies, urban research has engaged with the potential harbored by rural areas and small cities in light of the influx of the urban, creative, educated middle-class. The 2019 study "Urbane Dörfer" (Urban Villages) considers the prospects and challenges for the respective locations arising from this new trend, focusing on the combination of digital modes of work (among them coworking) and living in the country. The city-country migrations investigated in the study are not only propelled by rising living costs in metropolitan areas (push-factor); they are also influenced by a desire for more space, for green surroundings, "for a sense of the originary, authenticity, and artisanal production," and for a collective understanding of living and working (pull-factor).[17] Even so, the basic prerequisite for this new movement is still good technical infrastructure. Arguing in a similar vein, the 2020 study from the Bertelsmann Foundation concentrates on the potential for coworking in small towns and rural areas.[18]

While these new forms of working and living have gained in popularity over the last several years, the exodus from the small and medium-sized cities beyond major urban centers still looms large. These approaches can nevertheless offer clues to the development possibilities that are currently being discussed with great intensity, in view of the ramifications of the COVID-19 pandemic and the growing importance of working from home.

16   See ibid., 64–69.
17   See Berlin-Institut and Neuland21, "Urbane Dörfer: Wie digitales Arbeiten Städter aufs Land bringen kann" (Berlin, 2020): 6–7.
18   Bertelsmann Stiftung, "Coworking im ländlichen Raum. Menschen, Modelle, Trends." (Gütersloh, 2020)

It can be assumed that the small and medium-sized cities characterized by positive, or at least mostly stable, socioeconomic conditions are above all those whose central cores are becoming increasingly attractive. The same is to be expected for suburban district centers. For those smaller towns in rural areas located on the periphery, whose population numbers are clearly shrinking, the development potential is likely to remain low in the future as well, despite several isolated projects of interest.

To be sure, the COVID-19 pandemic is altering the fundamental prevailing conditions, and its enormous economic repercussions are hampering the sustainable internal development of small and medium-sized cities overall, as well as of the central areas of city districts. At the same time, the pandemic also presents opportunities to be deployed as a kind of trend accelerator in connection with digitalization, for example, by promoting decentralized office spaces or new business formats. Indeed, a considerable hastening of the structural change in retail outlined above is looming, which will make it necessary for actors in both planning and politics to engage more intensively with the development of the central cores of small and medium-sized cities.

Businesses should be encouraged to establish, for example, digital inventory-management systems and offer click-and-collect services not dependent on a single site, and an improved technical infrastructure should be promoted. Moreover, it appears essential to reinforce cooperative planning and management approaches that integrate business and real-estate owners as cultural and social actors. Thus an important coordinating function falls to the municipal authority. And it is above all small and medium-sized cities that can profit from these shorter bureaucratic paths.

In order to bolster the attractiveness of town centers and make them more inviting to spend time in, as well as to coordinate the measures involved in achieving these aims, municipal governments must allocate resources accordingly. But the various actors prominent in commercial, cultural, and civil life need to be involved, too. Supermarkets are crucial as anchor points. Once the provision of daily needs is secured, the likelihood increases that existing businesses and institutions will survive in the town center or that new

ones will locate there. Alongside restaurants, catering, and service
trades, other trades that benefit from personal contact, such as
repair cafés, can thrive.

It is the task of development management to conceive and implement digitally supported programs for retail, services, craft trades,
and food services—or combinations among them—for commercial
spaces that become vacant. If attractive coworking spaces can
be established, suburban centers and small towns, as well as
small towns in rural areas, will be able to profit from the growing
importance of mobile work. This model can become attractive to
more than just freelancers. Larger firms from a region outsourcing
a portion of their office workspace can cooperate to guarantee a
minimum utilization rate for a shared office and thus reduce the
costs of the different working locations (central company office,
home office, coworking space).

One can find several examples for civic engagement in the centers
of small cities. The citizen cooperatives in Münden and Holzminden
in Hannover demonstrate how regions with low real-estate prices
can rehab and repurpose empty or underutilized buildings.[19] While
the upper floors are occupied by residential units, the ground floor
houses retail, restaurants, culture, and skilled craft and trades, as
well as office work, coworking, and pop-up concerts.

Cooperation with property owners is the decisive factor for a
(re)vitalization of town centers. As such, it can be helpful when a
municipal authority avails itself of the possibilities to intervene that
planning law allows. For example, preemptive purchase rights or
temporary property acquisitions can influence development. In
addition, the particulars of urban-development law (redevelopment
law, urban-development funding) make it possible to have a much
stronger influence via construction regulations on the functional
stability of town centers than was previously the case. More mus-
cular interventions of the public purse into the real-estate and land
markets can also be used to envision newly arrived (or existing)
supermarkets as mixed-use concepts, combining them with
housing, spaces for daycare, medical facilities, or cultural centers on
upper levels of buildings—piggybacking, as it were, one off the other.

19   See Bürgergenossenschaft Mündener Altstadt eG, https://www.bg-hmue.de/de/index.
php, and Bürgergenossenschaft Holzminden eG, https://bg-hol.de/, both last accessed
February 22, 2021.

One fear is that the transformation to climate-friendly forms of mobility in suburban and rural small towns will only be implementable with great effort. Low population density means long daily commutes, and public transport continues to be a less attractive alternative to private vehicles. In order to ensure the improved quality of public spaces as destinations for spending time, cycle paths and walkable connections should be treated as of at least equal importance; e-bikes (including cargo bikes) should be promoted as alternative modes of transportation, and parking spots for private vehicles should be arrayed either behind or on top of the buildings so that new structures can be better integrated into the growing urban fabric. Here, too, there are now many positive examples.

For small and medium-sized cities in suburban and rural regions, opportunities arise through supply structures located close to where people live, digitally supported offerings of goods and services, and the boost that decentralized "office" work has enjoyed. If this potential is utilized, the advantages of appealing conditions for life and the environment will be able to balance out the disadvantages of a relative lack of diversity and a low concentration of professional and personal contacts. Nevertheless, a stampede into small cities is not on the cards for the foreseeable future. But stable or growing regions still have the potential to help safeguard "equivalent living conditions" in Germany.[20] This presupposes that politicians, government administrators, and private actors also seize on this potential. That these entities traditionally are well-acquainted with one another can be advantageous, but it can also present problems. Success will depend on whether or not the short routes within these places and structures can be utilized productively.

20   BMI, "Unser Plan für Deutschland: Gleichwertige Lebensverhältnisse überall" (Berlin, 2019).

Tired of the City

Harbingers of New Rural Commons

One of the narratives about the pandemic is that urbanity is in crisis. Rem Koolhaas, among the most influential theorists of the city since his 1978 book Delirious New York, sees in rural life a way out of the social impasse that he finds life in cities threatening to become: "We have allowed our core values to shift: from liberty, equality, and fraternity to a fetish for convenience, security, and sustainability." The inhabitants of cities, Koolhaas continues, have little sense of agency; shrugging one's shoulders has become the most common stance. In the countryside, by contrast, he sees more freedom of movement and room for improvisation.[1]

The statement strikes a nerve in our everyday life during the pandemic: life in the city is becoming increasingly cramped, and the countryside—until recently, often denigrated as provincial, backward, or inconsequential—is garnering new appreciation: more space for less money, with more nature, more open space. We do not yet have figures to determine whether urban fatigue is prompting urban flight to the country. Globally, as in Germany, it is movement to popular boomtowns that still dominates demographic flows. But during the pandemic, new spaces for action have suddenly opened up, unforeseen and unplanned, especially through digital working. A third of all employees in Germany have worked at home temporarily during the coronavirus crisis; even one-half would have been feasible.[2]

1   Mathias Alexander, "Freiheit statt Komfort," *FAZ*, March 12, 2021, https://www.faz. net/aktuell/feuilleton/debatten/architekt-rem-koolhaas-preist-innovationsgeist-in-afrika-17241851.html, last accessed August 2, 2021.
2   Jean-Victor Alipour et al., "Homeoffice-Potenzial weiter nicht ausgeschöpft," March 3, 2021, https://www.ifo.de/DocDL/sd-2021-digital-06-alipour-etal-homeoffice.pdf, last accessed August 2, 2021.

73 Never before have so many people been able to take their jobs to the countryside, nor have they stopped commuting every day to work in the city. For the discipline of urban planning, this places certainties into question and forces a reassessment and channeling of developments ranging from mobility and social participation to how we deal with land. The detached single-family house with a garden, which for ecological reasons had long since appeared to be a thing of the past, has grown more attractive since the beginning of the pandemic. In the green belt surrounding Berlin, the increase in demand has been as high as 75 percent.[3] And the German federal government is moving further and further away from its goal of limiting urban sprawl. Hence there is a need for alternatives to single-family homes, to new construction, to the reflexive zoning of new land for construction. Community living and working in existing buildings, which is still the exception on the housing market, could point the way to a new rural life that is socially and ecologically sustainable.

Countryside Cooperatives

While groups formed to realize joint housing projects and newly founded cooperatives have until now mostly been an urban phenomenon, large properties far from the urban centers are now also becoming attractive: farms and manor houses in need of renovation, disused industrial plants, abandoned military and railroad sites. Often, these are properties with existing buildings that have been vacant for some time: too large for a family or small group of people, too remote for classic project development, too bulky for conventional-use concepts. On the initiative of private individuals, and partly also under the aegis of foundations or urban housing cooperatives, more and more collective projects are emerging in the countryside. The clientele they interest, who often meet on cohousing platforms, could be prototypically sketched as follows: independent with a university education, willing to share (gardening, raising children, shared spaces, cars, and e-bikes), open-minded about new forms of living, and looking for community. The same opportunity that the high-income urban middle class saw twenty years ago in communal building projects in city centers is today the farm in

3   Sebastian Engelbrecht, "Immobilienentwicklung in der Pandemie: Von der Krise keine Spur," March 24, 2021, https://www.deutschlandfunk.de/immobilienentwicklung-in-der-pandemie-von-krise-keine-spur.766.de.html?dram:article_id=494661, last accessed August 2, 2021.

Community living and working in the countryside: Prädikow Farm, one of the largest four-sided farms in Brandenburg. Photo: Peter Ulrich

the countryside, ideally with a rail connection nearby. Roughly 6 percent of the population is interested in collaborative living and working, says Rolf Novy-Huy, executive director of Stiftung trias, a foundation: "It's the very young people. Or those facing a biographical change, those leaving a single-family home that had grown too large, and moving into a small, accessible apartment."[4]

Founded in 2002, the Stiftung trias is an anchor of the collective housing movement and, as a "nonprofit land developer," the antithesis of a commercial real-estate developer. It operates by acquiring land and making it available to community projects via leases. Housing projects can also apply for funds to support environmental and climate-protection measures. The conditions can be negotiated in individual cases; the only requirement is the use of ecological building materials and native plants. The foundation has gathered a good forty projects under its umbrella. Of the projects, 20 percent are new buildings, while 80 percent are conversions of existing buildings. Currently, the foundation no is longer supporting new construction.

So far, only a small proportion of the foundation's projects are located in rural areas. Community projects in large cities face fewer hurdles, Novy-Huy notes; in a village or on the outskirts of small towns, the critical mass of interested parties is lacking. But since the beginning of the coronavirus pandemic, he adds, it's clear that many are willing to move further out of the city, and that existing projects no longer have problems finding occupants for their space.

The Prädikow Farm in the region of Brandenburg known as Märkische Schweiz, or the Swiss March, is the Stiftung trias's rural showcase project: one of the largest four-sided farms in Brandenburg, with fifteen buildings formerly used for agriculture and nine hectares of land, under development since 2017 as a new location for living and working. The first residents will move in in 2021, and a total of one-hundred people are expected to live on the extensive site in the village of Prädikow, which has 250 inhabitants and is located about an hour east of Berlin's city limits. The land is owned by the foundation and leased to the Berlin tenants' cooperative Selbstbau e.G., which is gradually renovating and converting the building. The

Village Barn at the entrance to the site, completed in 2021, will be open to the whole village and guests with a pub, event spaces, and coworking spaces.

In Prädikow, there are flashes of the future of rural life, as in many places around Berlin. Shortly before the outbreak of the pandemic, the study "Urbane Dörfer: Wie digitales Arbeiten Städter aufs Land bringen kann" (Urban Villages: How Digital Working Can Bring Urbanites to the Countryside) examined community-oriented housing projects in the new German states.[5] Examples include rural cooperatives such as Uferwerk in Werder (Havel), with car-sharing, a repair workshop, and a food cooperative; Gut Stolzenhagen on the Oder River with guest house and cultural center; small communities with five to ten members and coworking spaces in renovated manor houses; and housing projects with artists' residences, as found for instance in a refurbished Plattenbau in Libken in the Uckermark region. For the most part, the initiatives use and expand the existing buildings, but there is also a new construction project, the Ko-Dorf in Wiesenburg (Mark), where, based on the model of vacation villages, a development with different types of houses, guest rooms, and coworking and community spaces is planned.

The concentration of projects in sparsely populated Brandenburg is due to the spillover of Berlin's cultural scene, which can no longer find affordable space in the capital's tight real-estate market. But housing cooperatives are also springing up in other German states, such as south of Munich, where battles over who has access to affordable housing have been fought for decades. While many large German cities are made up of a majority of single households, a return to community and the common good is being tried out in vacant monasteries. These are representative buildings, already built for large communities, with a past as cultural centers: what better way to redefine rural life?

Kloster Schlehdorf, a baroque complex with a secondary school and chapel on the shores of Lake Kochel in Bavaria, was sold in 2019 to Munich-based WOGENO, a cooperative umbrella organization for housing projects that has acquired or newly built twenty-five houses with around 830 residential

5   Berlin-Institut für Bevölkerung und Entwicklung/Neuland21 e.V., "Urbane Dörfer: Wie digitales Arbeiten Städter aufs Land bringen kann," August 2019, https://www.berlin-institut.org/fileadmin/Redaktion/Publikationen/PDF/BI_UrbaneDoerfer_2019.pdf, last accessed August 2, 2021.

units since it was founded in 1993. The remaining nuns of the Missionary Dominican Sisters have moved into a new building on the site, and the convent building itself is to be transformed into Cohaus Kloster Schlehdorf, a place for living, working, seminars, and events. The purchase was preceded by an eighteen-month phase of test living and concept development. The old building, with 300 rooms and a total of 10,000 square meters of space, will be home to six large cluster apartments and various temporary and permanent housing options, among other uses, in the coming years.

Such redevelopment of monasteries is only just beginning. Hundreds of Christian monasteries in Germany and Europe will be available for new uses in the coming decades, says Ulrike Rose, who co-founded the association Zukunft Kulturraum Kloster in Schlehdorf: "The number of sisters and brothers is steadily decreasing, churches are having to abandon large monastery buildings, and the few remaining religious congregations are being merged."[6] The new secular communities have yet to take shape and many questions remain unanswered. What are the rules that people want in living together? How should one deal with different levels of responsibility and presence in the community? How can the new residents (ideally) make a connection to the original social or spiritual mission of the monasteries? And how can housing remain affordable in historic, often listed facilities? The extensive common areas—hallways, commercial kitchens, prayer rooms—must be communally funded and used, and the bedrooms, former cells, are small. Privacy and the public sphere must be renegotiated, and these projects call for tailored architectural designs and use concepts.

Rural Islands of Urbanism

What many new projects in the countryside have in common is that they create social, cultural, or tourist infrastructure in addition to living and working space, in an attempt to become part of existing village and residential-development communities. Housing affordability and openness to the surrounding community are top priorities, especially for cooperatives. There is nonetheless a danger of new rural islands of urbanism: what we see emerging are networks of projects with links to Berlin, Munich, and other major cities, with urban habits and life models. Real-estate prices are rising because more urbanites are moving near to these rural clusters, often with second homes. Will rural life in the future become a luxury for digital elites? Will less-privileged groups of society soon no longer be able to afford this land, eventually forcing them to move to less desirable suburban locations? It's too early to speculate about such an outcome. But this makes it all the more important to promote integrative projects, to deal with land in a way that is oriented toward the common good, and to work closely with the municipalities so that the gentrification so familiar in cities is not repeated in rapid succession in parts of the countryside.

What these new rural projects also have in common is that they are mainly being realized in existing buildings and fit into existing structures, which reduces vacancies. In this respect, as well, they are the counter model to new constructions of single-family residential areas that are being developed outside deserted village centers or in areas between cities. Despite the climate crisis, the construction and building industry—responsible for almost 40 percent of CO_2 emissions globally, as in Germany—is still focused on new construction, on more living space, on growth. Dense housing projects with collectively used resources, which are more common for rural areas, offer models that are not only socially but also ecologically sound.

Trying Out a New Place to Live, with Broadband Internet Access

This new rural life is not yet a megatrend, in part because working digitally depends on the expansion of broadband Internet and mobile network connectivity, which is progressing only slowly in rural areas in Germany. Many who have grown tired of the city opt for a soft transition between city and country, for hybrid living models somewhere between a city apartment, a dacha, a guest room, and a second home. Commuting is done as needed, with the focus of daily life shifting from time to time and plans made for retirement. This sounds like privilege, but it doesn't have to, not least because cooperatives offer small spaces for little money. For municipalities, models for living between urban and rural areas are a challenge. Authorities are forced to adapt to residents who come and go, to changing responsibilities and needs, which means they can only loosely plan capacities for daycare centers, schools, and public transport, or estimate tax revenues.

From a religious to a secular community: Kloster Schlehdorf in a painting by Simon Warnberger (1769–1847). Photo: Wikimedia Commons

In the second year of the coronavirus pandemic, more and more communities are offering the opportunity to try out working and living away from the city, tailored to people looking to make a switch—because not all regions are experiencing new inflows of residents, and some have to work to make this happen. During a campaign called the Summer of Pioneers, for instance, people can live and work digitally in vacant houses for a few days or weeks in Homberg (Efze) in Hesse or Altena in southern Westphalia: on offer is an "all-round carefree package" with a furnished apartment, Internet connection, and access to specially equipped coworking spaces on brownfield sites that have the potential to be developed. Working together, companies, municipalities, and private relocation agencies are promoting remote locations and calling for volunteer engagement: "In 2021, you have a unique opportunity to work as pioneers with local people to usher in a new chapter in urban development."[7]

While the housing shortage is worsening in cities, houses and apartments are standing empty in many of Germany's 294 counties (as well as in many of its neighbor countries). Room to implement new ideas, which has to be fought for in the big city through grass-roots initiatives, is practically served up on a silver platter in smaller towns. And it is here, precisely, that many municipalities are not offering ready-made solutions but actively seeking out participation in decision-making processes. Just imagine what might happen if the many strategies for structurally weak areas that have been, and are still being, developed at international building exhibitions in this new millennium (IBA Urban Redevelopment Saxony-Anhalt 2002–2010, IBA Thuringia Stadtland, 2012–2023, IBA Fürst-Pückler-Land 2000–2010) were to find new resonance because of the pandemic and finally be realized: vacancy and conversion of existing buildings, experimental cooperation between government administration, business, and civil society, the revitalization of factories, the expansion of organic farming with direct sales to cities, the reopening of schools and daycare centers. If millions of people retain the option to work from home after the pandemic ends, and if major cities fail to respond quickly enough with affordable and flexible housing, rural life could look quite different in the not-so-distant future.

7   Stadt Altena/Neulandia UG, "Summer of Pioneers Altena," https://altena-pioneers.de, last accessed August 2, 2021.

From Coworking Space to Neighbor- hood Office

How Flexible Digital Work Could Alter Urban Districts

When the concept of coworking spaces migrated from the United States to Germany around 2009, its effect on the world of work was groundbreaking, offering a new vision of the future. The idea of flexibly sharing spatial resources and expertise within a community was seized on above all by self-employed individuals and start-ups in the creative and communications industry, who heralded it as a "new kind of working."

In contrast to shared office communities with long-term rental contracts, coworking spaces made it possible to rent a workstation under flexible conditions for the short-term, either as a designated space or one selected each day; the infrastructure of a typical full-service office, up to and including secretarial services, was part of the package as well. But not only that: coworking spaces offer access to a network whose activities extend beyond just having conversations on a break. Many offices organize events—some more, some less moderated—such as business breakfasts that are mainly communicated and advertised internally and thus promote networking within the respective office or community.

In recent years, the operators managing coworking spaces have swiftly become more professionalized and specialized, which has starkly limited the original openness of the concept. The growing choice of offerings has catered to the ever more specific spatial or material needs of the respective target audience. Coworking spaces have opened with photo studios, training courses for artists and programmers, childcare, or even overnight accomodation. In addition, coworking chains have sprung up with branches worldwide that are open to every kind of professional category but with high rents that mean they appeal above all to an established clientele or to startups with correspondingly robust financing.[1] The US-based firm WeWork rents workstations (working spaces) in stylish office environments at more than 700 sites in 119 cities. These spaces include club memberships and a variety of recreation options and are offered not only to individuals but also firms and teams with up to 500 employees. What began as a social idea has long since become a lucrative and oftentimes exclusive business model.[2]

Working from Home—From Blessing to Curse and Back Again

The beginning of the COVID-19 pandemic abruptly threw the practiced routines of the workplace into disarray. People and companies for whom traditional office work had always been conducted at a company's physical location, and who considered this a sort of natural state of affairs, were now confronted for the first time with the perks and drawbacks of working from home.[3] Many employers

1   This article is based on insights found in the following book: Agnes Katharina Müller, *Coworking Spaces: Urbane Räume im Kontext flexibler Arbeitswelten* (Münster: LIT Verlag, 2018).
2   In some places this led to coworking spaces contributing to the displacement of sociocultural life as the companies offering them leased or bought up properties that they then renovated and rented to a wealthier clientele.
3   See Hans-Böckler-Stiftung, "Studien zu Homeoffice und mobiler Arbeit," https://www.boeckler.de/de/auf-einen-blick-17945-Auf-einen-Blick-Studien-zu-Homeoffice-und-mobiler-Arbeit-28040.htm, last accessed February 16, 2021.

Coworking in Lisbon: Up to 250 freelancers, creatives, or digital nomads can rent workspaces on the gallery floor of the Mercado da Ribeira. A lounge with a café takes over the function of the reception. Photo: Iwan Baan

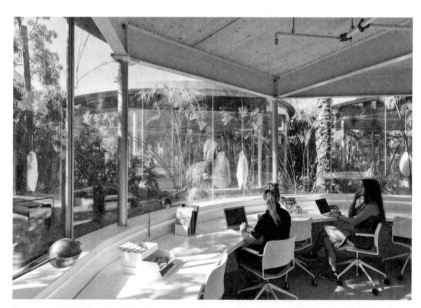

Coworking in Los Angeles: the sixty offices and meeting rooms include about 700 workstations in a garden-like atmosphere in the Hollywood neighborhood. Photo: Iwan Baan

found that their employees were also productive and motivated
outside the office and quickly announced their intention to integrate
mobile work into the work culture after the pandemic; employees
would no longer be required to come to the office every day but
rather only on specific days. Behind this plan lay not least the idea
of reducing office space and thus saving costs.[4] At the same time,
many employers recognized the advantages of time saved by cut-
ting out the commute to work and the ability of bringing work and
private life into better balance.[5] And yet working from home is not
a long-term option for many; indeed not everyone has a separate
office space at home, nor do they want to set up their laptops in the
kitchen or bedroom for the entire day.

Along these lines, the experience of working from home on the
part of both employees and employers could promote the further
development of coworking as a concept. Thus coworking could in
the future address not only the current clientele from the creative
industry and the self-employed but also all those who require an
office workspace outside their own four walls. Communal working
spaces in residential areas containing workstations with flexible
leases could offer workers an alternative to corporate offices
and apartments and could help them structure their workday.
By moving into empty retail spaces and serving as a gathering
place, thereby facilitating social contacts with the neighborhood,
workspaces could provide a boost to district centers. They could
assist in the reduction of commuter traffic and thus contribute to
realizing the "city of short distances" or the 15-minute city popular-
ized by Anne Hidalgo. They could enhance the prospects of a city
oriented toward the common good through salary-based and fair
rental prices for workstations, as well as through more varied use
concepts for spaces, in order to make these spaces accessible for
the entire neighborhood. But what exactly must these new, flexible,
communal office spaces accomplish, and where should they be
located?

4   See Jean-Victor Alipour, Oliver Falck, and Simone Schüller, "Homeoffice während der
     Pandemie und die Implikationen für eine Zeit nach der Krise," *Ifo Schnelldienst*, July
     2020, 30–36.
5   forsa Politik- und Sozialforschung GmbH, "Erfahrungen mit Homeoffice. Ergebnisse
     einer Befragung unter abhängig Beschäftigten in Bayern," *Ergebnisbericht*
     f20.0512/39563 De, Ma, https://www.dak.de/dak/download/forsa-umfrage-
     ergebnisse-2401560.pdf, last accessed April 4, 2021.

Coworking spaces have so far been located primarily in city centers, where those working in creative industries enjoy opportunities to have lunch and shop as well as good connections via public transport. These users harbor a strong identification with the image of their coworking location, which is often viewed as tantamount to a business address.

If coworking is to appeal in the future to those looking for a flexible workspace near their homes, it will be necessary to create offerings in residential districts. This kind of new coworking space must achieve something that neither the corporate office nor the home can provide. As a "third place" between kitchen table (first place) and company office (second place),[6] it must ideally be reachable by foot or bike in a matter of minutes and offer an atmosphere conducive to undisturbed work, far from roommates or family.

Converted parking garages, department stores, or warehouses are just as much candidates for coworking space in the established districts of large and midsized cities as infill development around existing building stock. Spaces in the crisis-plagued retail sector in district centers and on main roads are already being repurposed into offices. However, coworking spaces do not function solely to fill gaps in vacant properties. On the contrary: through their purchasing power, coworkers contribute to preserving the mix of existing restaurants and shops.

Coworking spaces aimed at artists in need of ample space have meanwhile also popped up in the suburbs of major cities or in rural areas. Those located in the countryside, which have frequently provided overnight accommodation, are now transforming this type of approach into an enduring paradigm for living and working. As soon as the law provides a framework for employees to only commute to the company offices one or two days per week, the trend towards living outside major cities will intensify.[7] Nevertheless, this change

---

6   See Ray Oldenburg, *The Great Good Place: Cafés, Coffee Shops, Bookstores, Bars, Hair Salons, and Other Hangouts at the Heart of a Community* (New York: Marlowe & Company, 1999).

7   Rental and purchase prices there are more reasonable than in the city, there is correspondingly more affordable space for living, and the proximity to nature is also more valued. Projects that test out living and working digitally in the country are already active, for example the Uferwerk in Werder (Havel).

The Hollywood branch of London-based coworking company Second Home opened in 2019.
The designs are by architecture firm Selgas Cano. Photo: Iwan Baan

has a prerequisite: good connections to the company office, ideally
with public transport.

In order for new coworking spaces to set up shop in new developments, they must be planned as part of the infrastructure along with local amenities supplying the community.[8] Instead of stipulating minimum parking space requirements for apartments, municipalities can enshrine a required workstation minimum in the local building ordinances so that a sufficient number are created in the immediate vicinity of residential buildings. Eventually, flexible layouts could in the long term improve the ability to adapt to changing needs.

Neighborhood Offices—New Roles and Collaborations

One rental criterion of coworking-space users is the community itself. When not only the rental prices but also the atmosphere and network suit them, many coworkers are prepared to accept longer journey times to reach the space. Coworking spaces have so far seldom had much interaction with the neighborhood around them; they are rather like islands in the district, isolated from their surroundings and yet at the same time globally networked with the coworking scene. Points of contact emerge during the lunch hour, as coworkers fan out among the neighboring cafés and restaurants, but inside the office the scene remains rather insular. Coworkers purposefully choose their workstation so as to encounter others similar to themselves and to swap expertise but also to be around others with whom they are, in matters of lifestyle, on the same wavelength. Some operators aim specifically to support such insular communities. Exclusive coworking spaces, often with more than 200 workstations, regulate access via club membership and erect additional, conspicuously visible, social barriers by means of distinctive entrances and concierges.

However, to ensure the success of coworking spaces in the future, open and barrier-free access for the neighborhood appears essential, whether that space is located in a village community or a newly built urban development. A public café connected to the work areas, a laundromat, or even a small library on-site would

8   In cooperative housing projects such as the Kalkbreite in Zurich, working spaces with flexible uses are being integrated into the site for residents.

be helpful in this regard and could contribute to the revival of the surrounding district. Such amenities would provide above all a boon to those who themselves cannot work in the spaces. This is an important gesture, since according to a study by the Ifo Institute for Economic Research on "Working from Home during the Pandemic and the Post-Crisis Implications," the ability to work from home is a perk enjoyed primarily by those with university degrees and high earners. Higher-qualified workers engage in more cognitive activities, work that can generally be shifted just as easily to the home.[9] The majority of workers, such a care workers, salespeople, or tradespeople, must continue to be present at a dedicated place of work.

Eventually, the offerings of coworking spaces and neighborhood centers would be combined and expanded to become new neighborhood offices. During the day, people will be working at their computers, but at night these sites can serve as venues for cultural events and meetings for clubs or seniors; and on the weekend family celebrations or workshops for children can take place. This would not only utilize the resource of space in a much better way than in the traditional company office, which in most industries sits predominantly empty outside of normal working hours. By day the new neighborhood offices could also tap into new target audiences and take on additional roles beyond providing space for work.[10] Young people could receive tutoring on-site or meet with their study groups and benefit from the working atmosphere in the office. Recent transplants to the area or even refugees could find a place to work in these spaces in order to prepare applications or take an online language course. Neighborhood offices would thus assume additional roles as integrators within the neighborhood. For things to function smoothly, though, on-site management would be necessary, similar to that in existing coworking spaces. This would coordinate the partly parallel uses of the space, tend to the needs and concerns of the users, ensure respectful interactions, and cultivate contacts, thereby setting the tone for a welcoming culture in the neighborhood office.

9   See Alexandra Mergener, cited in Alipour, Falck, and Schüller, "Homeoffice während der Pandemie," 32.
10   In their design for a workers' housing estate in Mulhouse, the French architect-duo Anne Lacaton and Jean-Philippe Vassal employed prefabricated greenhouses that could be used as a garage or a living space according to need.

The Lisbon branch of London-based coworking company Second Home opened in 2016. The designs are by architecture firm Selgas Cano. Photo: Iwan Baan

The question of the concrete location and specific scale of the
new neighborhood offices will be answered quite differently
depending on the particular needs of the surrounding area. Will the
residential community offer an additional workspace with an open
workshop where neighbors can repair things or children can learn
to do woodwork? Will empty business spaces in office towers be
converted into apartments with community spaces on the ground
floor for new residents that can be used by day as third-place
workplaces and by night as a meeting place for a singing club or for
gymnastics? Will empty factory floors provide space for work by
day and by night, with the desks for work "sent flying" and stored
in the ceiling, serve as a dance floor for tango events? One can
imagine many possibilities.

Hybrid Models—Financing and Integration

As appealing as this vision sounds, such a model with diverse
offerings and needs won't always function without conflict and will
be accompanied by negotiations between parties. This is especially
the case since the danger exists that particularly engaged users will
downright monopolize the site for their own activities and networks
and thus, similar to what occurs in coworking spaces, end up more
or less consciously uncoupling themselves from the neighborhood.
Simply making spaces available is not sufficient for successful
integration into the neighborhood and reduction in barriers to entry.
Thus the question presents itself: how can neighborhood offices be
realized and, above all, financed?

In order to ensure financing, it is necessary that employers help
cover the costs of workspaces located outside the company
offices. Businesses should in the future pay a percentage of the
cost of the external spaces that reflects the amount of time spent
working there. It could also be possible to peg the amount of rent to
the respective salary of the users in order to subsidize workspaces
for lower-wage workers and neighborhood activities.[11] Politicians
and government administrators need to facilitate here, through

11   The bUm space for engaged civil society in the Kreuzberg district of Berlin represents
        one such example of a coworking space. bUm also supports neighborhood meetings
        and organizations with spaces. Workspaces for nonprofit organizations are rented for
        one-quarter of the price paid by businesses. In addition, there is a midprice solidarity
        rate through which the less well-off can be supported.

regulations, such mixed uses in residential areas and to actively support the establishment of neighborhood offices. Coworking spaces have thus far only been promoted sporadically by local governments, the justification being that their operators are a commercial business. A prerequisite for municipal sponsorship is, as with many other initiatives, whether or not these spaces contribute to the public interest. Depending on the extent of communal activities planned on-site, the local authority itself could step up as a (co) operator of the space, or provide incentives for external operators, such as lowered commercial taxes, under conditions that specify the configuration and scope of offerings to the community.

With the help of a municipal subsidy, operators of coworking spaces already located in residential districts could open their offices to the entire neighborhood and offer differentiated rental rates or make the spaces available for communal activities at no cost. Branch-based companies could open subsidiaries with integrated satellite offices in residential districts and make these accessible to the entire neighborhood for working and communal activities. The businesses would certainly profit from such social engagement: they would increase their appeal as employers with their staff and moreover garner a positive social image.

Whether the local authorities themselves operate the neighborhood offices or whether they perform the role of partner or initiator—in any case they need a set of guidelines for configuring and using such neighborhood offices and a coordination center that identifies appropriate spaces, helps clarify questions pertaining to financing, and mediates between interested operators and real-estate owners or project developers. The goal should be for new neighborhood offices and their offerings to respond to local circumstances and needs in the spirit of a city oriented toward the common good without losing sight of the inclusive character of diverse groups of users. It remains to be seen what magnitude such neighborhood offices can accommodate so that the coordination of uses remains workable, as well as which of the different formats harmonize with one another and at what sites the neighborhoods can ultimately take advantage of these offerings.

Aglaée Degros, Sabine Bauer, and Markus Monsberger

Dividing Space Fairly

The Potential of Mobility Spaces to Repair the City

With the collaboration of Eva Schwab, Stefan Bendiks, and Jennifer Fauster

The confinement during the pandemic has reminded us that we live somewhere and not just anywhere.[1] Suddenly, we have (re)discovered our surroundings; we have realized that our cities are much more fragile than we thought. We can observe that the core districts of cities are becoming deserted; the accumulation of vacant spaces and shops is increasing rapidly; the residential districts lack basic amenities; our accommodations and flats are too cramped and our public spaces too tight. Suddenly, the dwellings in the city have become too expensive, the high density and compact texture uncomfortable. Suddenly? Really?

Discussions of urban density in relation to sanitary crises are not a recent phenomenon; they are more or less as old as town planning itself.[2] The relationship between density and the eradication of epidemics formed the basis of density regulations in the industrial city.[3] What we need to rediscover is the importance of combining quantitative regulations with qualitative ones. Looking back at history,

---

1   Bruno Latour, *Où suis-je? Leçons du confinement à l'usage des terrestres* (Paris: La Découverte—Empêcheurs de penser rond, 2021).

this has not always been this way: the Hampstead Garden Suburb is an example of how planning regulations helped define spatial quality. The recommended density was approximately twenty houses per hectare. Beyond that, a distance between houses of at least 16.5 metres, with gardens in between, was advised. Hedges, rather than walls, were used to separate the spaces. The streets were lined with trees, and green spaces were open to all. Affordable rents allowed for social diversity.[4] Nowadays, the way we develop our cities has resulted in a process that mainly occurs through negotiation between private and public actors. Density indicators are quantitative instruments used in such bargaining processes and have become less and less an instrument of spatial design and more a tool serving real-estate negotiation.[5] Our environment is affected as well; since its ecological and social qualities are not quantifiable, it is often missing in the city.[6]

According to the Organisation for Economic Co-operation and Development (OECD) report[7] Under Pressure: The Squeezed Middle Class (and its forerunner The Broken Social Elevator? How to Promote Social Mobility), one in three people from the middle class are economically vulnerable. This is due firstly to the automatization of labor and secondly to the rise of housing expenses. In 1985 in the twenty-four European countries of the OECD, a middle-income household with two children needed 6.8 years of annual income to be able to afford a 60-square-meter dwelling in the country's capital city or financial center; nowadays, nearly double that amount is needed. During the past twenty years, housing

2   History teaches us, as Philippe Rahm describes it in his works *Ecrits climatiques* and *Histoire naturelle de l'architecture*, about the close relationship between sanitary conditions and urban planning in different periods, including the Haussmann era. When the great boulevards of Paris were laid out, by definition a new space of mobility, they were intended as a measure to combat the cholera epidemic. But they were also the expression of a new order, namely that of the bourgeoisie. Haussmann took advantage of the epidemic crisis to create a novel vision of the city through new mobility spaces. See Philippe Rahm, *Écrits climatiques* (Paris: Edition B2, 2019) and *Histoire naturelle de l'architecture* (Paris: Editions du Pavillon de l'Arsenal, 2020), as well as Philippe Panerai, Jean Castex, Jean-Charles Depaule, and Ivor Samuels, *Urban Forms: The Death and Life of the Urban Block* (Oxford: Architectural Press, 2004): 35.

3   Meta Berghauser Pont and Per Haupt, *Spacematrix: Space, Density, and Urban Form* (Rotterdam: Nai010 uitgevers, 2010).

4   Philippe Panerai et al., *Urban Forms*, 35.

5   Aglaée Degros, "The Territorial Project," in *Basics of Urbanism*, ed. Degros et al. (Zürich: Park Books, 2021, in press).

6   Eva Schwab, "Die Grundlage des Städtebaus: Nachhaltigkeit und Gerechtigkeit im territorialen Projekt," in Degros et al., *Basics of Urbanism*.

7   OECD: *Under Pressure: The Squeezed Middle Class* (Paris: OECD Publishing, 2019), https://www.oecd.org/els/soc/OECD-middle-class-2019-main-findings.pdf.

prices have risen three times faster than the income of the average
middle-class household. The COVID-19 pandemic therefore
highlights the fact that the urban housing someone is able to afford
is often tight and undersized—especially if one is confined to it.
This shows that cities are more and more designed for speculation
rather than for human beings.

It is not only that our homes feel cramped; the urban texture of the
city, and more specifically its interstitial spaces (the space that
spans from façade to façade), also feel immensely tight during the
lockdown. Urban dwellers and agents of active mobility, e.g., pedestrians, often need to squeeze onto 80-centimeter narrow sidewalks,[8]
while the rest of the space is primarily dedicated to car traffic and
parking. Especially in the context of the COVID-19 pandemic, which
is manifesting itself in public space in the requirement to maintain
a minimum distance of 1.5 meters between people, such an inequi-
table distribution of space between different users seems like an
even more cynical form of ridicule than before.[9] Indeed, it questions
certain behaviours inherited from the 1950s. An illustrative example
is the ostensible logic behind the way public space today gives
spatial privileges to vehicular traffic—to both driving and parking
cars. The areas we concede to cars not only limit qualitative public
space in our cities but also reinforce the negative effects of climate
change (for example through a high degree of ground sealing). And
of course the cars themselves contribute to climate change through
their high emissions. The crisis exposes the problems inherent in a
modernist approach to public space dominated by car mobility, an
approach from which we must now emancipate ourselves.

The above shows that the fragility of the urban model has been
present for much longer than the COVID-19 crisis; current times
only highlight or accelerate it. Problems such as real-estate speculation, lack of quality in market-driven developments, and poor
use of space stem from long-entrenched urban-planning practices
governed by the imperatives of profit and growth. Within the last
several years numerous calls have been made for urban planning
that is not based on growth as mere consumption of space[10] and
that takes responsibility for social[11] or ecological[12] inequalities, or
both.[13]

8   Bernadette Redl, "Am Gehsteig: Zu wenig Platz für Abstandhalten," *Der Standard*,
        October 31, 2020, https://www.derstandard.at/story/2000121301274/am-gehsteig-zu-
        wenig-platz-fuer-abstandhalten, last accessed June 24, 2021.
9   Aglaée Degros, keynote at UNESCO City of Design Subnetwork Meeting, October 7,
        2020, https://youtu.be/pYzhEpnFlqo?t=460, last accessed June 24, 2021.

"Never waste a good crisis," Winston Churchill once said. Undoubt-edly it is time to act, because in the wider context of climate transition the problems mentioned above are likely only forerun-ners. The crisis presents us with the opportunity to implement a paradigm shift: repairing our environment and transforming it into a more ecological place, valorizing its natural elements, the air, the water. A space that lends itself almost as a matter of course to this change of paradigm is the one dedicated to mobility. This is a space still inherited from modernity and highly standardized by technocratic dictates. Although public space, by definition, should not be dedicated to the storing of private objects (vehicles) nor should it operate solely for the benefit of a particular type of user (drivers), it is in fact rarely perceived or treated as a true reserve of urban public space.[14] Since this resource is scarce and has to take on other important functions in terms of climate change adapta-tion and mitigation, active mobility is a good way to reduce land consumption for mobility overall and to be able to use the freed-up land for other purposes. In recent years, principles that allow for a re-appropriation of space have been developed and tested in various cities such as Barcelona, New York, and Brussels, demon-strating the immense impact of a revised approach to traffic space on the social and ecological sustainability of cities. The publication Traffic Space is Public Space sums up those strategies[15] and tools classifying them into six categories that guide the reclamation of traffic space: the transformation of its aesthetics, the creation of connections, participation, the sharing of space, the revitalization of the local economy, and metabolism help transform these spaces into truly public spaces.[16] The pandemic has especially affected the last four aspects. It can be observed that participatory processes were greatly reduced. Yet once social contacts are resumed, it is

10   Yvonne Rydin, *The Future of Planning: Beyond Growth Dependence* (Bristol: University Press, 2013).
11   Bernardo Secchi, *La città del ventesimo secolo* (Rome: Laterza, 2005).
12   Mohsen Mostafavi and Gareth Doherty, eds., *Ecological Urbanism* (Zurich: Lars Müller Publishers, 2016).
13   Bruno Latour, *Où atterrir ? Comment s'orienter en politique* (Paris: Éditions La Découverte, 2017).
14   Stefan Bendiks and Aglaée Degros, *Traffic Space is Public Space* (Zürich: Park Books, 2019).
15   Ibid.
16   Ibid.

In Barcelona, city and regional government departments have been working with residents to test how to reallocate street space in residential neighborhoods and how changing traffic patterns can create social interaction. The project Superilles (Superblocks) has been running since 2003. Photo: Ajuntament de Barcelona

likely that those processes can be restored. It is also more than
likely that the other three aspects (the sharing of space, the revitalization of the local economy, and metabolism) will undergo a structural transformation and that long-term changes will continue. The following remarks draw on a number of exemplary projects from around Europe to highlight the potential of recent changes in traffic space for improving the quality of urban public space. They present the most important learnings from the crisis and beyond.

Considering the Sharing of Space

The effects of the COVID-19 pandemic on bicycle and pedestrian mobility were evident in modal split data. In Vienna, both transport modes together increased from 35 to 46 percent. After a dip during the first lockdown in March and April 2020, car usage returned to the level seen before the crisis, while the use of public transport dropped and remains low. Passenger numbers showed significant declines and are now at about 60 percent of their former volume.[17] In the upcoming recovery phase, it is considered essential to enhance public transport by taking a long-term view and implementing more frequent connections, hygiene measures, simple ticketing for the entire route chain, and increased communication and public relations outreach.[18] Improving public transport is crucial in order to meet our climate goals, avoid traffic jams, and limit the space dedicated in general to mobility mainly by restricting the space consumption of the largest consumer, namely private car traffic. The crisis of public transport brings with it an increase in individual transport. It is now necessary to direct this individual mobility to active forms such as walking and cycling.[19] It is not only a question of waiting for collective mobility to recover but also of seizing the opportunity to improve active mobility networks. Some

17   Wiener Linien, "Rückblick 2020, Ausblick 2021," https://www.wienerlinien.at/web/wiener-linien/rückblick-2020-ausblick-2021, last accessed March 4, 2021.
18   VCÖ Mobilität mit Zukunft, "Öffentlicher Verkehr der Zukunft—Lehren aus Covid-19," https://www.vcoe.at/projekte/vcoe-veranstaltungen/detail/vcoe-veranstaltung-oeffentlicher-verkehr-der-zukunft-lehren-aus-covid-19, last accessed March 4, 2021.
19   Shibayama et al. "Impact of COVID-19 Lockdown on Commuting: A Multi-Country Perspective," in *European Journal of Transport and Infrastructure Research* 21, no. 1 (2021): 70–93, https://www.researchgate.net/publication/349212591_Impact_of_COVID-19_lockdown_on_commuting_a_multi-country_perspective; VCÖ Mobilität mit Zukunft, "Umfrage zeigt, wie stark Covid-19 die Mobilität der Österreicherinnen und Österreicher verändert hat," November 26, 2020, https://www.vcoe.at/presse/presseaussendungen/detail/vcoe-umfrage-zeigt-wie-stark-covid-19-die-mobilitaet-der-oesterreicherinnen-und-oesterreicher-veraendert-hat, last accessed June 24, 2021.

cities seized the moment of the (first) lockdown and reacted quickly by redistributing available street space (due to reduced car usage). Examples of temporary cycle lanes can be found all over the world. Berlin started in Europe with the first well-documented pop-up cycle paths. They were set up as construction sites and more or less spontaneously became pandemic-resilient infrastructure; some of them are now set up for permanent use. Traffic beacons have been replaced by fixed bollards and orange site markings by white, permanent ones.[20] In Milan, 35 kilometers of streets were transformed and active mobility was prioritized in an experimental way. With color and creativity, asphalt was given new meaning and the streets transformed into strade aperte ("open roads").[21]

These examples show us that pop-up bike lanes can be unique opportunities to rewrite the street space and replace it with something innovative, something long-needed. This stresses the fact that: the development of active mobility reduces the space dedicated to mobility in a simple way and frees it up for other uses.

Despite all of these temporary actions, we should also be thinking about long-term adjustments. In a survey conducted by VCÖ Mobilität mit Zukunft, about 1,000 Austrians were asked their opinion on how the use of transport will change after the current crisis. More than half of them expect to walk and cycle more and fly less in the long term as a result of the COVID-19 pandemic. Another 45 percent assume that the primary transport mode for trips might shift to cars. Concerning public transport, people assume a decrease in usage. From the perspective of climate-friendly transport, there is a serious risk that public transportation use will wane and individual transportation will emerge stronger from the COVID-19 crisis.[22] From these observations, we can conclude that if we want to reduce the space dedicated to mobility in the urban fabric, it is now necessary to improve the provision of mobility based on individual movement that does not rely on private car ownership.

20   Christoph Gunßer, "Stadtumbau für die Verkehrswende: Radverkehr statt Autos," *DAB Deutsches Architekturblatt*, July 30, 2020, https://www.dabonline.de/2020/07/30/stadtumbau-fuer-die-verkehrswende-radverkehr-autos-corona-pop-up-radwege/, last accessed June 24, 2021.

21   Laura Laker, "Milan Announces Ambitious Scheme to Reduce Car Use After Lockdown," *The Guardian*, April 21, 2020, https://www.theguardian.com/world/2020/apr/21/milan-seeks-to-prevent-post-crisis-return-of-traffic-pollution, last accessed June 24, 2021.

22   VCÖ Mobilität mit Zukunft, "Repräsentative Befragung von Österreichs Bevölkerung zu Covid-19 und Öffentlicher Verkehr," November 2020.

This includes pedestrian mobility and all kinds of cycling mobility but also car-sharing systems. The crisis made room for a challenge to the highly normalized world of road infrastructure. The perpetuation of temporary actions will essentially depend on the legal possibility of transforming them into permanent designs by changing the system of infrastructure standardization itself. As an example, Brussels has temporarily adapted its city center—the Pentagon district—during the crisis in May 2020. The maximum speed limit was reduced to 20 kilometers per hour in order to prioritize quality of life and safety. The transformation into a traffic-calmed neighborhood allows pedestrians to use the full width of the street and not just the sidewalks. This has given people more space, reducing also the risk of contagion.[23]

As a consequence of these positive developments, the entire car network had been permanently slowed down in January 2021, following long-standing plans. This reduces noise pollution and increases road safety, and not only in the inner city.[24]

A comparable strategy is described in the latest edition of the Zurich handbook for street planning ("Standards Fussverkehr"[25]), where a shift from a "center line out" to an "outside in" organization of the street is suggested, building on the city of Toronto's "Complete Street Guidelines." This means that instead of designing a street's profile to meet the needs of (car) traffic in the center, it should be expanded from the edges according to the needs of life and use.[26]

23   City of Brussels, "Adjustment of the Pentagon Residential Area," https://www.brussels.
      be/residential-area, last accessed June 24, 2021, last modified February 15, 2021.
24   City of Brussels, "Brussels 30 km/h Zone since 1 January 2021," https://www.brussels.
      be/brussels-30-kmh-zone-1-january-2021, last modified January 4, 2021.
25   Stadt Zürich Tiefbauamt, "Standards Fussverkehr," 2020, Schweiz, online under:
      https://www.stadt-zuerich.ch/ted/de/index/taz/verkehr/verkehrskonzepte.
      html#fussverkehr, last accessed May 31, 2021.
26   City of Toronto, "Complete Streets Guidelines," https://www.toronto.ca/wp-content/
      uploads/2017/11/906b-Chapter-1.pdf; https://www.toronto.ca/services-payments/
      streets-parking-transportation/enhancing-our-streets-and-public-realm/complete-
      streets/complete-streets-guidelines/, last accessed March 4, 2021.

The COVID-19 pandemic has boosted the digitalization of work and commerce alike. A survey conducted by TQS on behalf of VCÖ regarding teleworking in October 2020 states that working from home was possible for around two-thirds of Austrian employees. Half of them have been teleworking more frequently since the outbreak of the pandemic. Seventy percent of respondents expect a long term increase in teleworking arrangements and online meetings.[27] Companies that operate globally (such as Allianz, Siemens, Google, or Facebook) also expect an increased use of teleworking even after the end of the pandemic.[28]

Teleworking and home-schooling solutions became considered a necessity and could be understood as the ground zero of mobility. But teleworking has not contributed to a reduction in the negative environmental impacts of high-commuter car use,[29] as a rebound effect was observed. It has been shown that measures to reduce mobility (e.g., commuting) may lead to an increase in other types of mobility (e.g., recreational travel) or a shift to less environmentally sustainable modes of transport. Both may negate or mitigate the potential climate impact of reduced commuting,[30] as everyone has a more or less stable "mobility time budget." The time that people spend on mobility every day is therefore constant on average, irrespective of changing framework conditions, because "saved" time is in turn spent on (other) mobility.[31]

27   VCÖ Mobilität mit Zukunft, "VCÖ: Zwei Drittel der Beschäftigten können Home-Office arbeiten – die Hälfte davon ist infolge von Covid-19 häufiger im Home-Office," November 6, 2020, https://www.vcoe.at/presse/presseaussendungen/detail/vcoe-zwei-drittel-der-beschaeftigten-koennen-home-office-arbeiten-die-haelfte-davon-ist-infolge-von-covid-19-haeufiger-im-home-office, last accessed June 24, 2021.

28   Johannes Reichel, "Greenpeace-Studie: Homeoffice könnte Millionen Tonnen CO$_2$ sparen," September 23, 2020, https://vision-mobility.de/news/greenpeace-studie-homeoffice-koennte-millionen-tonnen-co2-sparen-65685.html, last accessed June 24, 2021.

29   Giovanis Eleftherios, "The Relationship Between Teleworking, Traffic, and Air Pollution," *Atmospheric Pollution Research* 9 (2018): 1–14.

30   Rudolf Scheuvens, "Was kommt da auf uns zu?–Digitalisierung in Handel und Industrie," in the university course Smarte Quartiersentwicklung in kleinen und mittelgroßen Städten, Graz 2019.

31   Haselsteiner et al., "Zwischenergebnisse/Zusammenfassung: mobility4work—Mobilität für die digitalisierte Arbeitswelt," 2020, https://projekte.ffg.at/anhang/5eba23d3a663d_mobility4work_zwischenergebnisse_zusammenfassung.pdf, last accessed March 4, 2021.

The routes not taken to work are therefore replaced by other
trips, some of them of necessity (e.g., for shopping) and others for
leisure. To avoid this rebound effect, it is crucial to have an urban
environment equipped with the basic functions for existence at
close distance, thus making car usage obsolete. This stresses the
fact that if teleworking is to have an impact on mobility reduction, it
needs to go hand in hand with the "proximity city." Already before
the pandemic, some cities had developed and promoted plans of a
fifteen-minute city. The underlying idea of the fifteen-minute city
is that of chrono-urbanism, which aims for a decentralized urban
structure. Following it, each neighborhood is equipped with local
suppliers, doctors, open spaces and recreational areas, sports
facilities, shared offices, schools, childcare facilities, etc. All urban
functions necessary for meeting daily needs are thus accessible
within a quarter-hour on foot or by bike from anywhere in the city.
Accordingly, the connections are no longer provided by car-dominated streets but rather by public spaces that have enough
space for active forms of mobility and that provide high-quality
amenties.[32]

The city of Paris has already committed to such developments.
Besides traffic and environmental benefits, officials are confident
that they will be able to create more socially sustainabile cities
with vibrant community life through such chrono-urbanist tactics,
providing not only environmental benefits through traffic mitigation
but also economic benefits for retail and services.[33] In the course
of these developments, Paris is to be transformed into a green
city with short distances and fewer parking spaces and cars. To
achieve this ambitious goal, 60,000 inner-city parking spaces are
to be removed and replaced by green spaces, playgrounds, and
bike paths.[34] This means that every second-surface parking space
will disappear. The majority of the remaining parking spaces will no
longer be in public spaces but in garages. In the entire urban area
(with the exception of the Périphérique ring road), the maximum
permitted speed for cars will be reduced to 30 kilometers per hour.
Most inner-city trips are to be carried out on foot or by bicycle;

32   Stefanie Eisenreich, "Paris auf dem Weg zur Stadt der 15 Minuten?," January 2021,
      https://www.goethe.de/ins/fr/de/kul/dos/nhk/22079262.html, last accessed March 4,
      2021.
33   Alois Pumhösel, "Auf dem Weg zur 15-Minuten-Stadt," *Der Standard*,
      October 26, 2020, https://www.derstandard.at/story/2000121064251/
      auf-dem-weg-zur-15-minuten-stadt.
34   Eisenreich, "Paris auf dem Weg," 2021.

for driving, preference will be given only to logistics, commerce, and people with reduced mobility.[35] This vision of the city was one factor in the reelection of the mayor of Paris, Anne Hidalgo, in the midst of the pandemic, demonstrating the sensitivity of the urban population to the theme of proximity.

Considering the Metabolism

At the beginning of the first lockdown in Belgium, at the end of July 2020, the Belgian public health institute published a series of cartographic representations depicting the concentration of COVID-19 cases by commune (district) within Brussels, which showed the economically deprived districts as a territory in which the population is particularly exposed to the virus. These maps clearly lead us to understand that the quality of living conditions (cramped/overcrowded housing) is a factor favoring transmission.[36] But it is important to remember that although housing is the raw material of the city, it cannot be approached in an autonomous or isolated way. On the contrary, it must be thought of in articulation with other spaces (the street and the district), and thus one must keep in mind that those districts are also severely lacking in green spaces. During the time of limited mobility in the COVID-19 pandemic, the influence on physical and mental health of access to nearby green and recreational space became even more apparent.[37]

At the same time, people's desire to move away from the city into "greener" suburbs has risen, therefore boosting potentially non-sustainable settlement patterns. Within the urban fabric, open and green space contribute considerably to the quality of housing. A greater amount of qualitative open spaces can thus also represent an alternative to small-scale suburban residential areas.[38]

35   Vereinigung für Medienkultur, "Für die 15-Minuten-Stadt: Paris hebt 70.000 Parkplätze auf," October 29, 2020, http://www.medienkultur.at/neu/fuer-die-15-minuten-stadt-paris-hebt-70-000-parkplaetze-auf/, last accessed June 24, 2021.
36   Comité Scientifique du Logement (CSL), "Le rapport du Comité Scientifique du Logement est disponible en ligne," February 16, 2020, https://perspective.brussels/fr/actualites/le-rapport-du-comite-scientifique-du-logement-est-disponible-en-ligne; Selim Banabak et al., "Stadt/Land: Wo kommt es zu den häufigsten Covid-19-Ansteckungen?," Der Standard, February 1, 2021, https://www.derstandard.at/story/2000123711480/stadt-land-wo-kommt-es-zu-den-haeufigsten-covid-19.
37   Christine Geserick et al., "Lebenssituationen und Wohntrends in Österreich," 2016, https://www.ssoar.info/ssoar/handle/document/58009, last accessed March 4, 2021.
38   Julia Jarass, Neues Wohnen und Mobilität: Präferenzen und Verkehrsmittelnutzung in einem innerstädtischen Neubaugebiet (Berlin: Springer VS, 2018).

This stresses the fact that the transformation of the mobility space
is part of the ecologization of the city. Following the desire for a
greener and more livable city, an initiative titled 17 Grüne Meilen
(17 Green Miles) was established in Graz. It pursues the goal of
transforming at least one street in each of Graz's seventeen municipal districts into qualitative public spaces that meet the requirements for ecological and social sustainability. The transformation
is to be achieved through a reorganization of the street profile,
prioritization of bicycle and pedestrian traffic, and the integration of
elements that increase the quality of time spent in the space. These
elements were collected, examined, and categorized according to
their function ("green modules," "hydrological modules," "modules
of lingering," and "other modules"—these include lighting, shading
elements, and bike-parking possibilities) and expected effects on
the microclimate (cooling, air-quality improvement, unsealing) in
the context of a research project (Green Miles Graz). The resulting
toolbox of various elements serves as a guide for the development
of those green miles.[39]

In Vienna, on the other hand, the need for fast action was recognized and addressed through temporary street-cooling actions
in the summer of 2020. According to an "Urban Heat Vulnerability
Map," the areas where cooling was most urgently needed were
identified and eighteen "cool streets" were created. This enabled
targeted measures like the installation of water playgrounds for
children and shaded benches where older people could linger, put
their shopping bags down, and have a chat. In total, 698 pieces of
furniture were set up, along with forty additional small trees and
ninety planting pots; in additon, turf was laid out and water features
with vaporizing effects were installed. This led to measurable
improvements in the microclimate represented in a climatic study
of those spaces.[40]

39   Die Grünen, "Judith Schwentners Plan: 17 Grüne Meilen für Graz," July 8, 2020, https://
      graz.gruene.at/themen/umwelt-und-tierschutz/judith-schwentners-plan-17-gruene-
      meilen-fuer-graz; Daniela Mrazek, ed. Stadt Graz/Umweltamt (2021): "Grüne Meilen
      Graz," https://www.umweltservice.graz.at/infos/andere/Gruene_Meilen_Graz.pdf.
40   Stadt Wien, "Coole Straßen sorgen für Abkühlung," https://www.wien.gv.at/verkehr-
      stadtentwicklung/coolestrasse.html, last accessed March 4, 2021.

The streets were temporarily closed to motorized traffic and transformed into lively outdoor spaces that encouraged social interactions. According to a survey, the majority of Viennese inhabitants approved of this project. As a result, the city decided to transform four streets permanently into Cool Streets Plus in 2021 using tree plantings, asphalt in lighter colors, and shading or water elements.[41]

In Brussels, a commission dealt with how to improve housing quality as a result of the effects of the pandemic in economically deprived neighborhoods. One of the recommendations was to develop strategies for landscape structures at the neighborhood level, or even to integrate the parameter "relationship to green space for all new housing" in a housing development's initial design phases.[42] As an example of how this can be effectively implemented, the city of Brussels and the office Artgineering are working in the district of Haren, where a network of landscaped active mobility infrastructure that leads to nearby green spaces is being marked out and, above all, prereserved within the transformation being wrought by real-estate development of the district.[43] This entails the initial work of identifying, in a very precise manner, the natural spaces of quality both in the private and public domain—continuous vegetation, areas of forests, and gardens of a certain size—as well as identifying the potential connections to be made in order to gradually move toward a complete network.[44]

The aim here is to value green space both in its systemic and recreational role by increasing areas of contact between housing and landscape while at the same time creating corridors of biodiversity.

We can conclude that home-based work and the development of active mobility make it possible to reduce the space dedicated to mobility if we avoid the rebound effect and provide enough amenities in proximity to where people live. The recovered space allows us to ecologize and requalify the city, to make it fit for future

41   Stadt Wien, "Coole Straßen Plus," https://www.wien.gv.at/verkehr/strassen/coole-strassen-plus.html, last accessed March 4, 2021; Streetlife Wien, "Coole Straßen," https://www.streetlife.wien/coolestrasse/, last accessed March 4, 2021; mobilitätsagentur wien, "Die Straßen kriegen Hitzefrei," https://www.mobilitaetsagentur.at/coolestrasse/, last accessed March 4, 2021.
42   CSL, "Le rapport du Comité Scientifique du Logement."
43   Artgineering, "Vademecum aménagement et signalisation des sentiers et chemins de Haren," project description (not published); Bruxelles (2020): "Dénomination des chemins et sentiers de Haren," https://www.bruxelles.be/denomination-des-chemins-et-sentiers-de-haren, last accessed April 15, 2021.
44   CSL, "Le rapport du Comité Scientifique du Logement."

developments and challenges. The crisis we are experiencing can therefore be seen as a moment to be seized so that we can establish a new relationship between the space for mobility and the urban vision.

Beyond the City

Additionally, we can observe that teleworking may also be an incentive to choose a residence at a greater distance from the workplace, thus lengthening one's commute, even if it is not driven daily.[45] Real estate in suburban locations is currently in high demand, but up to now the idea of the proximity city was exclusively applied in central areas of the large European cities. If we do not want to perpetuate and amplify the problematic effects of sub- and peri-urbanization, the proximity-city approach also needs to be extended to smaller conurbations.

Such an approach can be observed in the idea of Leefbuurten (Living Neighborhoods), launched in 2021 by the Flemish minister Bart Somers together with the Team Vlaams Bouwmeester, Fiets-beraad Vlaanderen, and the Agentschap Binnenlands Bestuur, based on an inititial research project by Artgineering and VUB. The aim is to challenge and encourage sub- or peri-urban municipali-ties to make a leap in the quality of the design of public spaces in residential neighborhoods. A Living Neighborhood is designed with pedestrians and cyclists in mind. It is healthy and pleasant to live in, enables encounters among individuals who are moving on foot or bycicle, offers more space for relaxation and greenery, and meets ecological requirements. The call aims to bring new concepts into the discussion that align with the new paradigm: the choice of residence is no longer made according to the location of one's workplace but rather is influenced by the question of where one wants to live.[46]

45   VCÖ Mobilität mit Zukunft, "Home-Office Anteil in der Generation 50 Plus am höchsten," March 12, 2020, https://www.vcoe.at/presse/presseaussendungen/detail/ home-office-anteil-in-der-generation-50-plus-am-hoechsten, last accessed June 24, 2021.

46   Vlaamsbouwmeester, "Leefbuurten," project description, https://www. vlaamsbouwmeester.be/nl/subsite/leefbuurten, last accessed March 4, 2021; Vlaamsbouwmeester, "Buurten met lef, buurten vol leven," https://vlaamsbouwmeester. be/sites/default/files/uploads/Brochure%20Leefbuurten_46blz%20%2B%20 cover_1012_web.pdf, last accessed April 15, 2021.

111 Hence, if we do not want to continue the social and spatial fragmentation in urban peripheries, we must act and propose an urban model that shows care for the fragility of the city and that allows the lack of qualitative space and nature to be tackled. Our spaces for mobility must cease to belong to a world of consumers of resources and become part of a world of repairers. The former continue to develop the extractive economy by refusing to acknowledge global warming and the related crisis, while the latter seek to recreate a weaving of territories by patching: they repair, fix, and rebuild a damaged world.

David Sim

The *Soft City* in Hard Times

How Public Space Proved Itself in Denmark

113 In 2019, my book *Soft City* was published.[1] The subtitle *Building Density for Everyday Life* might sound like the worst possible for life in 2020 and 2021, in a world dealing with a pandemic. *Soft City* is about convivial urban *hygge* and people enthusiastically participating in public life. With COVID-19, it has been all too easy to envisage a harder, colder, urban future environment, with a culture of physical distancing, favoring the safety of individual travel in private motorcars, seeking seclusion in suburban, detached houses or even splendid isolation, high up in concrete towers.

Now as we emerge from the pandemic, I want to revisit some of the themes and concepts in the book and relate them to the post-COVID-19 city, hopefully provoking some thought, as we collectively embark on reimagining and redefining our cities to meet new needs and behaviors.

But this is not just about my own feelings. Everyone has opinions, based on their own personal experiences. However, in the midst of the lockdown and after, Gehl (the company where I work) went out and surveyed what was actually going on in the public realm of Danish cities, to find out where people were and how they were engaging and interacting. With the support of Realdania and the city of Copenhagen, and with more than eighty surveyors in four cities in Denmark, we observed how streets and public spaces, parks and playgrounds, served the very unique needs of our communities during the pandemic.[2] What we learned was heartening. Not only has the importance and value of public spaces been demonstrated during the pandemic, but they bode well for the future of urban life, allowing emerging patterns of new behavior, proving the value of living locally and of soft mobility, contributing to physical and mental health.

Denmark, like many countries, had a lockdown with large parts of society closed, including schools, civic and cultural institutions, and workplaces, resulting in almost everyone spending more time at home indoors. When the Danes did go outside, it was most often for buying groceries and other essentials, taking a walk, or exercising. By surveying life in public spaces, we learned that while there was

1   David Sim, *Soft City: Building Density for Everyday Life* (Washington, D.C.: Covelo, 2019).
2   Gehl's research on public life during the COVID-19 pandemic can be found at https://covid19.gehlpeople.com/.

a significant drop in the classic city center commercial activities, in their place there was more recreation, exercise, and play. In fact the amount of use of public space was more or less the same as before, although mobility had decreased significantly.

While overall mobility decreased in the city center, pedestrian movement increased in neighborhoods outside of the city center. In particular, local places that already offered a public activity (such as a playground) were even more popular than before. Notably more children and—this is significant, given their vulnerability during the pandemic—more older people used the city's public spaces than before. It would seem that the basic needs of being outdoors and being among other people became even more valuable.

After lockdown, this redistribution of users in public spaces continued with more children and elderly present. And the local neighborhoods, which gained popularity during lockdown, continued to do so. The neighborhoods that offered a mix and diversity of amenities seemed to be more frequented, with more play and exercise activity. The number of people talking to each other in public spaces increased, and people seemed to be more likely to reach out to strangers. Although more people were using cars, walking and biking increased even more.

So already, I can say that I don't think the COVID-19 pandemic spells the end of urban life as we knew it. In fact, I suspect it's quite the opposite. In many ways, the pandemic has reinforced many advantages and the value of living in cities—at least if they are "soft" cities.

Less Space, More Time

Our lives are framed by space and by time. The human-made constructs around these phenomena contain—and constrain—our everyday. With the pandemic, we suddenly had much less space to contain our daily lives and yet more time to spend in that smaller space.

Not all cities are like Copenhagen, which in typical soft Scandinavian democratic style has been making continuous and consistent investment in the public realm over the past sixty years. Across the planet, the pandemic was not an equalizer in society, and it has exposed much of what we should have already known. There is certainly little equity in space and its distribution. The quality and quantity of space in the private sphere almost always reflect financial wealth. And the (financially) better off have certainly been better off physically during the months of lockdown, thanks to the comfort of larger living spaces and the flexibility of their lifestyles.

In addition to this, the differences are further exasperated by the fact that homes with greater private amenity are frequently in the neighborhoods with better public amenity including more spacious public spaces—a major factor in decreasing the risk of contracting the virus through social contact. On the other end of the socioeconomic scale, the adverse is true, with spatial and social restrictions exacerbating fragile urban lifestyles with more confined dwellings and more limited access to quality public spaces.

Time is something you might expect to be more democratic. To start with, everyone has just twenty-four hours a day to spend regardless of wealth or social position. However, it could be argued that those who have to work longer hours for less money are more likely to have to be present at their physical workspaces, as well as to travel further to get to there. And they are the same ones who live in homes and neighborhoods with less amenities.

The City of Minutes

Living locally has proved to be a luxury, and I think the recognition of this might explain the recent worldwide fascination with the much vaunted 15-minute city. The convenience of physical proximity is not just about space. It also contains the gift of time. Within the idea of the 15-minute city, I think there are smaller fractals of urban life: the 1-minute city, the 3-minute city, and the 5-minute city.

Jan Gehl often refers to the far greater value of a square meter of useful space right outside your front door, compared to 100 square meters of park a few blocks away. This always made me think of the hyperlocal: the considerable value of the edge zones or soft edges of buildings that are less than a minute away, or the coexistence of two very different worlds, such as the quiet, enclosed courtyard thirty seconds away from the busy street; or the small details like the continuous pavement or the median strip which allow you to cross the street spontaneously, without a time-consuming detour.

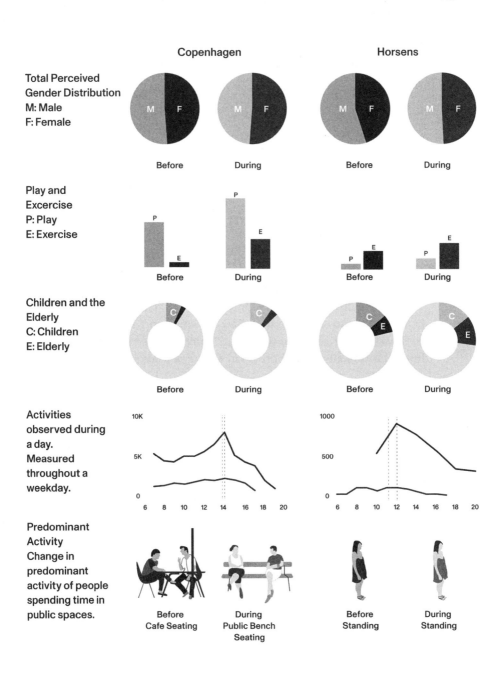

Copenhagen   Horsens

Total Perceived Gender Distribution
M: Male
F: Female

Before   During   Before   During

Play and Excercise
P: Play
E: Exercise

Before   During   Before   During

Children and the Elderly
C: Children
E: Elderly

Before   During   Before   During

Activities observed during a day. Measured throughout a weekday.

Predominant Activity
Change in predominant activity of people spending time in public spaces.

Before   During   Before   During
Cafe Seating   Public Bench   Standing   Standing
                Seating

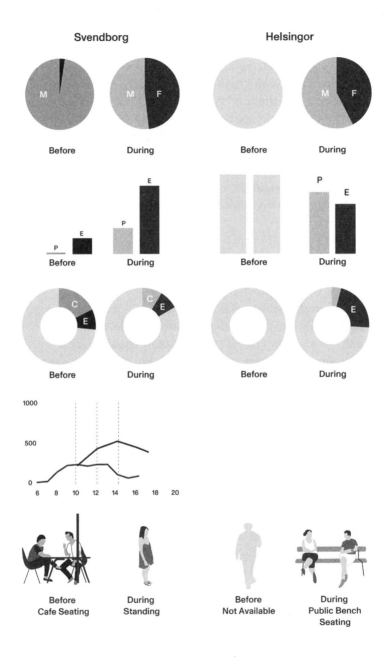

Svendborg

Helsingor

Before   During

Before   During

What these seemingly banal details allow is for hyperlocal life to take place. It takes you just fifteen seconds to bring your laptop and coffee cup to the back garden or the balcony to experience a totally different work environment alfresco. Children can be playing outside with their friends in the safety of the back courtyard within forty-five seconds, while you (and other parents) look on as you cook dinner (of course, it might take more than forty-five seconds to get them in again once the food is ready). In a similar way, buying fresh bread might take just three or four minutes if the bakery is literally on the corner of your block. Waiting for the bus can be a pleasure when the street is filled with useful shops and services, or well-dispositioned benches. The wait can easily become a sponta-neous and welcome coffee break, a sun-soaked rest, or a friendly chat. In this way, precious minutes can even become delightful moments.

Urban Form That Connects Us

And it is here that my inner urbanist stepped in, as I observed how the physical make-up of our surroundings invited or inhibited neighborliness. This is often banal stuff, about the position of a window or the placement of a door, the organization of apartments around a common staircase, or the presence of a balcony. These simple phenomena can enable spontaneous invitations and serendipitous encounters in the vicinity of the home.

One simple example is the significance of streets. It has become clear that streets as physical spaces can do more than accommo-date cars. With thoughtful prioritizing and redistribution of their limited surfaces, they enable more soft mobility, provide useful space for doing business, and offer much-needed recreational space. Additionally, the analog urban pattern of traditional streets is often reflected in virtual groupings for organizing help between neighbors, demonstrating that a neighborhood is not just a place but also a state of mind.

Around the world, despite the challenges of the pandemic, we have seen the benefits of living in cities, especially if they are "softer" cities. The following observations are some soft urban phenomena that make a big difference to the functioning and the quality of life in locked-down cities, and at the same time offer clues to how we might make better cities in the future.

Among so much tragedy, some of the most optimistic images during the pandemic came from one of the worst-affected areas in the world. Few could have missed the charming balcony scenes from Italy. The balcony is something so simple, and really rather affordable; just a few square meters of concrete or wood, yet offering service for hundreds of years, physically connecting people every day to fresh air, sunshine, and the outside world. Compare this with the high cost and short life of a motor car, or even an appliance like a TV or a computer.

And alongside balconies, there are the other soft-edge zones: porches, verandas, vestibules, bay windows, front steps, and stoops. All of these act as useful buffers between inside and outside, bridging between public and private, often providing those vital 2 meters required for physical distancing. But importantly, these architectonic buffers work two ways, not only physically in distancing, but to enable proximity, sociability, and even intimacy. These range from the practical aspects of leaving a parcel on the porch or dropping the groceries on the front steps, to truly delightful experiences such as offering a place to sit out, to enjoy the weather and feel connected to the rest of humanity, while still staying safely at home.

Soft Urban Form: The Value of Walk-up Buildings

In a similar fashion to the simplicity of the balcony, the common staircase of a traditional walk-up apartment building creates a resilient microcommunity, one that regulates and manages many of its own affairs and cares collectively for its own members. It enables daily staircase encounters, offering some eight, ten, or twelve households to be continuously updated and aware of each other's lives, making for trust and common understanding—for keeping an eye on the old lady on the second floor, knowing who to ask to borrow a bottle of milk (or wine), children feeling there are other adults they can get help from if a parent is absent.

In terms of polite physical distancing, the common staircase is intuitively negotiable. You can open your apartment door and you can listen to find out if anyone is there or anyone is coming: you can simply hear if the coast is clear. In the same way, once you

The graphics were created as part of the study "Public Space Public Life COVID-19," which was carried out in 2020 by Gehl in four Danish cities. Graphic: Gehl

120

Several local destinations see increased use during COVID.

Sundbyøster Plads in Copenhagen has twice as much activity on the weekend in April 2020 in comparison to a December weekend day in 2019.

Same flow of people on Amagerbrogade Later peak time— 14.00, 17.00

Key:

New activity during COVID

Activity, which remained the same

Activity not present during COVID

Different age group

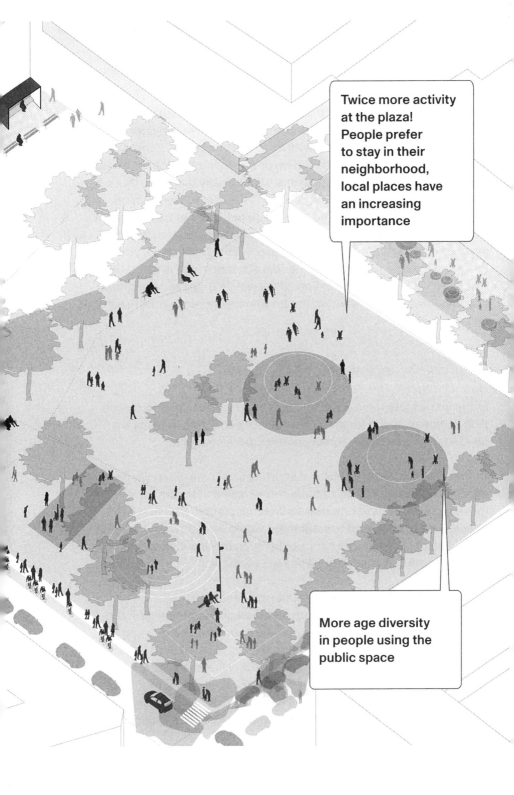

are moving through the staircase, you can hear doors opening,
behind you or in front of you; you can slow down or speed up. Of
course, the shared acoustic space allows for greetings and small
exchanges of useful information.

In comparison to the stairs, taking the elevator is like Russian rou-
lette during a pandemic. Cramped and confined, the elevator itself
is an unsanitary box of germs with its infectious buttons and surfaces. There is no natural ventilation or sterilizing sunlight to kill the
virus. In the elevator, it is impossible to physically distance; there
is no room for the polite, small maneuvers and side steps which
are possible on the stairs. Of course, you might try to travel alone
in the elevator, but this creates an inherent confrontation with the
inevitable distrust of other elevator users. The doors open, you see
there is someone there. Your potential elevator-mate is a potential
disease carrier—not the most convivial way to meet your neighbor.
In comparison to the elevator, the traditional staircase is both safer
and more convivial.

Soft Mobility: The Value of Walking

Some basic facts forced major cities to reconsider the priority and
distribution of space for mobility when for economic reasons we
needed to get societies and economies working again.

During the pandemic, public transport was not safe when filled to
capacity. Probably one-third full is more realistic for safe travel,
meaning thousands of commuters were displaced. If all these
people took private cars to work there would be total gridlock in our
cities, and of course more cars would mean more pollution, which is
unacceptable in a respiratory disease pandemic.

Walking and cycling are the cheapest, cleanest, and most
space-efficient means of moving people while maintaining physical
distancing. Importantly, they require the cheapest and most rapidly
deliverable infrastructure. Walking makes physical distancing easy.
Pedestrians intuitively self-regulate. The individual has total control
to negotiate with other people as they make their way through the
city. And at the same time, walking allows individuals to choose their
own pace, their own route, and when to stop, look, and linger. In this
way, walking empowers the individual.

A Japanese friend told me about how she discovered independent mobility when she abandoned the risky, crowded carriages of the Tokyo metro and, for the first time, walked to work instead. It was the smartest option, and she found out that a forty-five-minute walk is surprisingly doable. This was a discovery in itself. And if the walk to work was doable, suddenly a whole range of other urban destinations with similar distances became possible, and the city became negotiable in a whole new way, totally independent of a timetable, completely free of charge and totally virus-safe. And along the way, apart from some much-needed exercise for free, there was a whole city of sensory experiences and useful services to be discovered—cherry blossoms and sunshine, shopping and coffee. And every day the route and the pace of the journey could change. Rather than arriving sweaty and stressed, my friend arrived at work refreshed and inspired.

Soft Places: More Public Space

The value of public space, of parks and gardens, streets and squares, can never be underestimated. Even though landscaping costs a fraction of what buildings cost, these outdoor spaces have always proved to be good investments and are a critical component of what makes the valuable "location" of a neighborhood.

Again, around the world we have seen road surfaces being turned into public space, giving confined citizens a place to get fresh air and exercise and to have social contact at safe distances and providing children with desperately needed play space. This kind of conversion has also helped the economy of local businesses, allowing people to wait outside shops while space inside was limited, and for café and restaurant terraces to spread out, compensating for lost space inside while still allowing physical distancing between the tables.

Balconies and back gardens, staircases and street trees, pavement extensions and cycle lanes are simple, low-cost, and low-tech solutions to the complex challenges of urban life. It strikes me that so many of the urban phenomena that gave us better-connected lives in the hard times of the pandemic (as well as in the good times before and after) are not necessarily expensive, complicated, or energy intensive.

The pandemic exposed many flaws in the make-up of modern society, and some of these failings reflect the unsuitable physical urban form of the built environment. With this in mind, maybe we might start to reimagine our cities, with more of the simple, soft details that better connect people to planet, to place, and to other people, and that make living locally not just possible but actually more attractive.

In this way, the amenity of the soft city is not only relevant during a disaster but even in normal times. Thoughtful soft solutions can help deliver a healthier, more sustainable, and more equitable world. And because these solutions are not expensive, it does not take much imagination to envision a city where everyone could have access to pavements and play space, balconies and bike lanes. As Jan Gehl frequently says, "It's cheap to be nice to people."

The End of Urban Life—Or Just the Start?

With the sudden change in the distribution of the time and space that frame our lives, the COVID-19 pandemic has given us an opportunity to value our precious time on our precious planet.

We might recognize that we can do more with less. We don't need to consume as much to live full lives; we don't need to travel as much. If we use less energy and resources in our everyday lives, we will spare the planet from unnecessary stress. If we need less money for our day-to-day tasks, we will save ourselves unnecessary stress. While there might not be dolphins swimming in Venice's canals (yet), the planet certainly seems to be doing better while we stay still, and in a similar way, this slower, more connected, local life might be good for us too.

125 Despite the many challenges, I believe that the future for human habitation on planet earth is urban. However, I suspect post-COVID-19 urban life will be more in the here and now, more time at home and living more locally—with more of our everyday stuff being done on foot or on a bicycle in our neighborhoods. Jaime Lerner, the Brazilian architect and mayor, famously said: "Cities are not the problem, they are the solution." Even after a pandemic, I still think that this holds true, if after these hard times we can recognize the value of soft cities. Urbanism can give us optimism.

Philipp Stierand

Three Meals Away from Anarchy

Cities between Food Security and Nutritional Poverty

Stacked chairs, cordoned-off patios, improvised counters for food to go: these are the images of the pandemic that will stick in our memories. Urban life had already made food a restless, roving matter before the pandemic, but now we are even more painfully aware of it: cities lack spaces where consumption is not compulsory, places that invite one to linger, where takeaway meals can be enjoyed. The COVID-19 pandemic (or better, the attempts to fight it) has brought changes to how we get our food. Other developments run more in the background or will only become visible in the future: market share has shifted among businesses, social problems have reached a new pitch, and weak points in the food system have been laid bare.

These unexpected developments are impacting cities, where civil society, policy, and government administration have only just begun in the last few years to grapple with the issue of food supply. The move to view the food system as a whole, and as something that falls within the purview of municipal politics, has often emerged out of an interest in urban agriculture. What fields of action, approaches to problem-solving, and new modes of questions emerge for food policy as a consequence of this starting point?

Pandemic-Related Upheaval in the Food Supply

Though the spring of 2020 saw store shelves cleared out by panic buying and, depending on COVID-19 regulations, consistently long lines in front of supermarkets, the pandemic did not fundamentally compromise the viability of our food supply. The system was sufficiently robust and flexible to respond to the stresses the pandemic placed upon it, and it continued to fulfill its function of providing sustenance without interruption. Nevertheless, having to give any thought at all to the functioning of the food-supply system was surely a new experience for most people living in Germany.

The food-retailing business was one of the few sectors that even managed to profit economically from the situation. With the disappearance of eating out, people working from home, and the closure of schools, retail enjoyed a marked increase in revenue (+11 percent compared to the previous year).[1] Overall, it appears that people eating at home have standards for food quality that exceed what they find when eating out. The growth experienced by discount supermarkets was in fact below average in 2020 (+8.8 percent), whereas sales at organic shops increased 22 percent. Direct-to-consumer marketers were the big winners within the organic foods sector.

By contrast, the food-service industry was one of the sectors most impacted by long closures. City life during the pandemic was sprinkled with the orange- and turquoise-colored backpacks of the food delivery services. This could presage an enduring shift of profits away from restaurants themselves: indeed, Lieferando, with a near monopoly on the delivery business, doubled its profits in the first

---

1 See Henryk Hielscher, "Lebensmittelhändler freuen sich über 'das beste Jahr seit Menschengedenken,'" *Wirtschaftswoche*, January 29, 2021, https://www.wiwo. de/26865642.html, last accessed March 30, 2021.

half of 2020. Wolt, a new competitor in the market, availed itself of the changing dynamics brought on by the pandemic to expand its reach from Berlin to Munich and Frankfurt. These delivery services utilize aggressive marketing strategies, copying the websites of existing restaurants; some use so-called ghost kitchens, marketed virtually as restaurants. Both approaches simulate urban diversity and thus compete with real diversity in the city.

The pandemic also provided a push for supermarkets to use delivery services. Such services had not had much luck in Germany in the past, and compared to the United States or Great Britain they clung to a meager share of the market. Residential areas remain generally well served by grocery stores nearby, and the delivery situation in an apartment complex is less than ideal; walking to the market is thus often more convenient than waiting around to receive an order. It is possible that it was the pandemic that gave the delivery services their big break in German cities. Gorilla, a delivery service founded in Berlin in 2020, had already collected a billion euros from investors after a mere ten months. In the third quarter of 2020, revenue for all food delivery services was 52 percent higher than it was the previous year.[2] It remains to be seen in the future how far the shift towards organic food and direct marketing and away from brick-and-mortar retail will go. That consumption habits will in part undergo lasting changes and thereby hasten larger processes of change impacting on our cities is, however, quite probable.

It can also be observed that food prices in Germany went up in 2020, increasing by 2.4 percent.[3] A reduction in sales tax in the second half of the year softened these increases. Above all, fruit (+7.1 percent) along with fish and meat (+6.1 percent) became markedly more expensive. During the first lockdown, fruits and vegetables were at times up to 10 percent more expensive than the previous year. This was due to factors that included interruptions in the supply chains caused by border closures and a shortage

2   See Lebensmittelpraxis, "Umsatzsprung bei Lebensmitteln," https://lebensmittelpraxis. de/handel-aktuell/28655-e-commerce-umsatzsprung-bei-lebensmitt eln-2020-10-05-08-58-09.html, last accessed March 30, 2021.

3   See AMI, "Lebensmittel sind 2020 teurer geworden," https://www.ami-informiert. de/news-single-view?tx_aminews_singleview%5baction%5d=show&tx_ aminews_singleview%5bcontroller%5d=News&tx_aminews_ singleview%5bnews%5d=23616&cHash=c3014d85ccae6d13f615837eba3dd67f, January 14, 2021, last accessed June 29, 2021; dpa, "Verbraucherpreise 2020: Energie war billiger, Lebensmittel wurden teurer," *Wirtschaftswoche*, January 29, 2021, https://www. wiwo.de/26830754.html, last accessed March 2021.

of foreign workers in the agricultural sector. Global food prices also rose in 2020: the FAO food price index is at its highest level in years.[4]

Public discussions have frequently focused on individual risk factors for COVID-19; conditions notable for an increased risk of a severe case of the illness include diabetes, cardiovascular disease, and being overweight, with poor diet as an important cause. At the same time, a strong immune system helps the body defend itself against diseases. Against this background, dietary supplements have experienced a veritable boom. Sales of vitamin C rose 94 percent in the first quarter of 2020 in comparison to the previous year's first quarter.[5]

Nutrition Councils and Local Food Biotopes

Even before the pandemic, the EAT-Lancet report observed that food systems have the potential to support human health and sustainable development, but that currently they present a threat to both. The discrepancy between positive potential and negative impact has become more than clear during the pandemic, and not only in relation to the question of health. At the level of the city, the question is how these contradictions can be resolved to the benefit of sustainable urban development.

In the past, municipal governments appeared to lack strategies for shaping nutrition policy at the local level; today, those governments are more and more responsible for conceiving and implementing the solutions for the ecological and socioeconomic problems of nutrition systems. The Milan Urban Food Policy Pact[7] and the Food Systems Network of C40 Good Food Cities[8] attest to the readiness

4   See FAO, "FAO Food Price Index," http://www.fao.org/worldfoodsituation/foodpricesindex/en/ (n.d.), last accessed April 3, 2021.
5   See Arne Hillienhof, "Nahrungsergänzungsmittel immer beliebter," *Wirtschaftswoche*, August 25, 2020, https://www.aerzteblatt.de/nachrichten/115926/, last accessed April 3, 2021.
6   See Walter Willet et al., "Food in the Anthropocene: The EAT–Lancet Commission on Healthy Diets from Sustainable Food Systems," *Wirtschaftswoche*, 393, no. 10170 (February 2, 2019): 447–492.
7   The Milan Pact is an agreement between cities around the world that commit themselves to developing sustainable food systems that are inclusive, resilient, safe, and diverse. Over 200 cities have already signed on.
8   C40 is a network of the world's megacities that have dedicated themselves to addressing climate change. Ninety-seven cities, comprising more than 700 million inhabitants, are active in the network. The Food Systems Network supports citywide efforts to create and implement an integrated food policy that reduces greenhouse gas emissions, increases resilience, and improves the health of the population.

and capacity to act on the part of local governments. With their examples of best practices and networks such as these, cities have been able to influence both national and European policy initiatives through their approaches to problem-solving.

One of the keys to designing a food system at the local level is considering the system as a whole, beyond the competencies and borders of particular disciplines. Only such an approach makes it possible to see potential solutions, and to recognize synergies and opportunities for action. Urban food systems aim to create a local biotope of best practices. These new local approaches typically integrate a diverse array of policy areas and goals that are con-nected both directly and indirectly with the theme of nutrition. An integrated approach has the potential to contribute to sustainable development, reinforce the regional economy, generate more employment opportunities in the food business, protect the areas surrounding cities, reduce CO_2 emissions, and cement trust in the food system. On an international level, programs of action that address the topic of nutrition (nutritional strategies) and specially focused institutions (commissions on nutrition or food coordina-tors) have proved to be effective tools for this policy.

In what follows, three themes will be discussed that have gained particular relevance in the preceding months: food security, the social influences on provisioning food, and the health of the city population.

Food Supply and Security

There is a saying of unclear origin: cities are only three meals away from anarchy. If provisioning mechanisms were interrupted from the outside, the city's inventory of food would last for one-and-a-half days. Then chaos would ensue. For coddled consumers accustomed to expecting full shelves ten minutes prior to a shop's closing, the inventory problems sparked by panic buying were both striking and upsetting.

The political reflex to close national borders starting in April 2020 precipitated enormous stress on the supply chains for food. Closed borders hardly hold back a virus (particularly when it is already circulating on both sides), but they do disrupt the flow of goods and workers, which in Germany resulted in price increases. In particular, the reliance of the agricultural sector on Eastern European workers become exceedingly clear. With rising concern in spring 2020 that the regional asparagus harvest could end up remaining in the fields, a centrally planned campaign was spearheaded to fly in harvest hands from Poland. The precarious working conditions in both the agricultural and food-retail sectors became even more visible during the pandemic. COVID-19 outbreaks in worker accomodation during the harvest made headlines. Operational shutdowns triggered by the infections of slaughterhouse workers led to massive disruptions in the specialized processing of pork, not to mention the lockdown of entire cities.

Optimized for efficiency, the food industry manages in normal times to ensure cheap food prices for urban residents, but during the pandemic this system suddenly had a negative impact on food provisions. There isn't really a backup supply system available to cities.

The resilience of a food system (and systems in general) can be captured in the following indicators: the capacity to withstand disruptions, the degree of interchangeability between elements, their flexibility and adaptability, and the speed with which they regenerate themselves.[9] Resilience is an elementary component of sustainability: without the ability to withstand short-term disruptions, there is no long-term viability. The resilience of food systems must occupy a more central position in discussions of future agricultural and food policies, especially in the face of an impending climate catastrophe.

One of the big problems with our food system with respect to resilience is its lack of variety. The agricultural and food sectors, from field to shelf, and from countryside to city, are marked by monocultures and near monopolies. New plant species account for 66 percent of global agricultural production, a mere eight species of animals are used by the meat industry, the gene pool of animals used in the production of meat and dairy trace back to just a few species (and a few corporations), and four companies dominate global trade in agricultural commodities.[10] Things don't look any

9   See D. M. Tendall et al., "Food System Resilience: Defining the Concept," *Global Food Security*, no. 6 (October 2015): 17–23.

10   See FAO, *The State of the World's Biodiversity for Food and Agriculture*, ed. J. Bélanger; D. Pilling; D. Pilling, *FAO Commission on Genetic Resources for Food and Agriculture Assessments* (Rome: 2019).

For more than 130 years, fresh food has been sold at the Mercado Da Ribeira in Lisbon. In 2014, the west wing was redesigned and expanded to include a food court with about thirty restaurants. The market activity can be observed through the windows of the coworking space on the gallery floor, which opened in 2016. Photo: Iwan Baan

better for urban commerce. In the German food-retailing industry, five large companies command almost 76 percent of the market.[11] But monocultures and monopolies generate a susceptibility to disruptions. Local food policy appears at first glance powerless against such global structures, but upon taking another look, it becomes clear that it is precisely the small-scale, local, regional alternatives that are the supplements needed to enhance resilience. Herein lies the strength of local food policy.

One starting point for more variety and redundancies is the promotion of ecological agriculture in the region. These practices support biodiversity in the field; they both facilitate and demand more diverse cultures; and they supplement national, European, and global commodity flows. Cities can stipulate ecological farming practices on their own lands, utilize organic products in their communal catering, and promote regional and local structures of commerce. Encouraging regional supply chains provides an alternative to long supply chains with global standards and highly processed products. Municipalities can use advice and information to connect local actors, promote their sales in (community) restaurants, and make their food a local brand. With the project Kantine Zukunft, for example, the state of Berlin is showing how the sale of regional organic foods can be promoted in community catering as part of a nutrition strategy. The project supports canteens and other establishments with intensive advice on how to further develop their offerings toward the goal of at least 60 percent organic food and more seasonal food from the region. In Berlin's free school lunches for elementary school students, an organic share of 50 percent is mandatory as of August 2021. The project Where Does Your Food Come From? mediates between school caterers and regional farms and provides educational materials.

The expansion of small-scale independent trade and craft processing counters the strong concentration of corporations in trade and industry with local alternatives. Cities and municipalities can support these more resilient structures by relieving them of what is often bureaucratic red tape and making these professions more attractive to successors, for example, through better training and image campaigns.

11   See Deutscher Bauernverband, "Situationsbericht 2020/21," https://www.
       bauernverband.de/situationsbericht/1-landwirtschaft-und-gesamtwirtschaft-1/15-
       lebensmittelhandel-und-verbrauchertrends, last accessed March 2021.

135 The resilience of a system also includes the economic security of its actors, which ensures that the economic situation in times of crisis does not lead to the failure of system components. A secure food supply thus also requires not only that it profit a few, but that all workers (from farm labor to crafts to trade) have a robust basis for work. Municipalities must keep this in mind when taking action: cheap food has social as well as health and environmental side effects and limits the security of supply.

Food Poverty

In the pandemic, some of the social problems on the producer side of the food system have made it into the headlines. The social problems in the city on the consumer side rather less so. At the latest since the introduction of the Hartz IV reforms to the German welfare system in 2005, social scientists have suspected material and social deprivation in the area of food for poor households. Yet the magnitude of the problem remains largely unexplored for Germany. The Scientific Advisory Board of the Federal Ministry of Food and Agriculture has come to the same conclusion: "In Germany, too, there is poverty-related malnutrition and, in some cases, hunger, as well as limited sociocultural participation in the area of nutritional needs."[12]

The crisis exacerbates these social problems. From a resilience perspective, difficulties arise when malnutrition or reliance on charitable organizations is tolerated even outside of situations of social crisis. There is a lack of capacity, for example, to buffer price increases or canceled school and daycare meals.

The first and most important step at the city level is to stop ignoring the problem of poverty-related malnutrition. The social aspects of food supply on the part of consumers must be given much greater focus. Everyone must be able to obtain sufficient supplies of good food.

12   WBAE – Wissenschaftlicher Beirat für Agrarpolitik, Ernährung und gesundheitlichen Verbraucherschutz beim BMEL, "Politik für eine nachhaltigere Ernährung: Eine integrierte Ernährungspolitik entwickeln und faire Ernährungsumgebungen gestalten," expert report (Berlin: 2020).

Social security systems are not within the sphere of influence of municipalities, yet there are local opportunities for action. The Scientific Advisory Board mentioned above is calling for special attention to children and adolescents in low-income households, as (early) childhood stresses are particularly damaging and for-mative. Family, daycare centers, and schools are the crucial living environments here.[13] Cities can influence healthy eating through daycare and school meals. In addition, the topic of nutrition must be an integral part of educational and social work and belongs in every neighborhood development. Here, nutrition can also play to strengths beyond the acute elimination of problems, because eating is an experience that connects all cultures and religions, all classes and milieus. Shared experiences around food are a means to combat the dissolution of social bonds and isolation, and to boost public spirit and cohesion.

The Healthy City

The public has (almost) become accustomed to the idea that our behavior and personal freedoms depend on the numbers of patients and utilization of intensive care beds. It has been strange to see, amid the current worldwide healthcare crisis, that author-ities have encountered little resistance to lockdowns ordering people to stay at home, while no one dares to advise people to pay attention to a healthier lifestyle—for fear of discussions about bans. Ultimately, the number of dead and seriously ill, and hence the accompanying restriction of basic rights, together with the magni-tude of economic damage in the current pandemic, also depends on the general health of the population. And here, nutrition is one of the decisive factors.

In Germany, two-thirds of men (67 percent) and half of women (53 percent) are overweight, and a quarter of adults are obese.[14] The risk of developing COVID-19 is 46 percent higher for obese people. Obese people who develop COVID-19 have a 113 percent increased risk of being hospitalized, a 74 percent increased risk of being admitted to the intensive care unit, and a 48 percent

13   Ibid.
14   See RKI, "Übergewicht und Adipositas," https://www.rki.de/DE/Content/
        Gesundheitsmonitoring/Themen/Uebergewicht_Adipositas/Uebergewicht_
        Adipositas_node.html (n.d.), last accessed March 30, 2021.

increased risk of dying.[15] "Currently, two pandemics are colliding," medical experts note.[16]

Promoting healthy eating must therefore also gain importance at the city level. In addition to the educational and social work mentioned above, communities can make healthy eating an easy and first choice at events, as well as in urban spaces. An environment must be created in which good nutrition is easy. Community food establishments are of particular importance here, and not only because municipalities have direct influence in many areas, but also because it is possible to help positively shape eating at home and in the food market, in addition to providing good food.

Food Policy: Municipal instead of Global

For municipalities, in the past there has seemingly been a lack of need to address nutrition policy: the population appeared to be well supplied. It is only in recent years that municipalities have returned to the issue of food supply. The reasons lay primarily in individual and social demands for nutrition beyond a basic supply. Prior to the pandemic, the new urban demands were primarily in the areas of trust in the quality of supply, and in the importance of environmental impacts, in health outcomes, and in fairness in the supply chain. The experience of the COVID-19 pandemic may bring the focus back to the basic functions of food supply. The dislocations described above have sharpened awareness for the performance and social equity of the food system; new attention is being paid to the resilience of food systems. Climate catastrophe and its projected impacts on agriculture and extreme weather phenomena will cause more frequent disruptions, in addition to permanent changes. For these developments, it is important to build food supply that not only does its part to avoid climate catastrophe, but that can cope with such disruptions in terms of climate impact adaptation.

---

15   See Barry M. Popkin et al., "Individuals with Obesity and COVID-19: A Global Perspective on the Epidemiology and Biological Relationships," *Obesity Reviews*, 21, no. 11 (2020).

16   Christina Hohmann-Jeddi, "Zwei Pandemien prallen aufeinander," *Pharmazeutische Zeitung* (December 2, 2020), https://www.pharmazeutische-zeitung.de/122118/, last accessed March 30, 2021.

Diversity and regional structures are the components that are
particularly lacking in our food system trimmed for economic efficiency. It is in these issues that the strength of community nutrition
policy is evident: decentralization is difficult to organize centrally.
Coupled with social and health issues, many of which also require
decentralized input, and the pressing problems of climate change,
the COVID-19 pandemic has once again underscored the need for
community food policy. Urban planning must understand urban
agriculture, food crafts, and commerce as essential elements
of sustainable infrastructure. Urban-development concepts are
faced with the task of integrating nutrition into goals and measures
alongside traditional topics such as housing or mobility. The aim is
not only to remedy weaknesses in the food system and minimize
damage but also to exploit its potential for urban development.

Emergency Urbanism

Los Angeles and Structural Racism in City Politics

Los Angeles is on the brink of one of the largest mass displacements in the history of the region. When eviction courts reopen,
nearly half a million renter households, concentrated in Black and
Latinx neighborhoods, will be at risk of expulsion through unlawful
detainers, or eviction filings—UD-Day is here.[1] In a deal struck with
the landlord and banker lobbies, the California legislature has put
forward tenant protections that postpone some evictions, keeping
tenants in a state of permanent displaceability. In a cruel hoax, such
protections convert unpaid rent into debt, turning the small-claims
court into yet another arena of violence against working-class communities of color. Los Angeles is the paradigm, not the exception.

Writing from Los Angeles, I interpret the present conjuncture as
emergency urbanism—the suturing of the ongoing "state of emergency" that is global racial capitalism with the declaration of emergency by the postcolonial state under the sign of public health. The
most obvious manifestation of a public-health emergency is the
COVID-19 pandemic and its racialized maps of infection and death
that make visible the disposability of Black, Brown, and Indigenous
life. But COVID-19 is conjoined with other takings of life. Patrisse
Cullors, co-founder of Black Lives Matter, explains the state of
emergency thus: "That Black folks across the country and the globe

---

1   UD-Day refers to the UCLA Luskin Institute on Inequality and Democracy report by Gari
     Blasi: https://challengeinequality.luskin.ucla.edu/2020/05/28/ud-day-report/, last
     accessed August 20, 2021.

are systematically targeted, and that our lives are on the line on a daily basis, and, that, ultimately, this is a life and death issue for us."[2]

The state of emergency has always been here. In Los Angeles, as well as in other US cities, working-class communities of color are subject to what I call "racial banishment," the enactment of their expulsion and disappearance from urban life.[3] It would be a mistake to understand such processes as gentrification or eviction, in other words, as market-driven displacement, for they are part of the through line of the forced removals of people of color. Racial banishment is state-organized violence, instituted through regimes of racialized policing, such as gang injunctions, nuisance abatement, and place-based surveillance.[4] Taking place in the name of the state's police power to protect the "free use of property" and ensure the "comfortable enjoyment of life and property," such forms of policing secure dispossession and enable formations of settler urbanism.

The Black Lives Matter uprising seeks to make such racialized policing and the dispossession of life untenable. Alongside such uprising in the streets, a reconfiguration of the social and spatial arrangements that make up urban life is also underway. In particular, property has become the insurgent ground of emergency urbanism, a site of rebellion against global racial capitalism and its protocols of rent and debt. The question at hand is whether such emergency presents the opportunity for a radical reconfiguration of the relationships among sovereignty, life, and property that are so central to American liberal democracy.

On May Day, amid the eerie quiet of the COVID-19 shutdown, activists with Street Watch LA, a tenant-rights coalition, staged the occupation of a suite at the Ritz-Carlton Hotel in downtown Los Angeles. The key protagonist, Davon Brown, one of the nearly 70,000 unhoused Angelenos, had been until then living in a tent in Echo Park Lake, a public park that has been the site of

2   Jamil Smith, "Black Lives Matter Co-Founder: 'We are in a State of Emergency,'" *New Republic*, July 20, 2015.
3   Ananya Roy, "Dis/possessive Collectivism: Property and Personhood at City's End," *Geoforum*, vol. 80 (2017).
4   Ananya Roy, Terra Graziani, and Pamela Stephens, "Unhousing the Poor: Interlocking Regimes of Racialized Policing," White Paper for the Square One Project, Columbia University, 2020.

WHAT IT TAKES TO MAKE A HOME

What It Takes to Make a Home, 2019
29 minutes, Canada, digital film
First film of a three-part documentary series
Conceived by Giovanna Borasi
Directed by Daniel Schwartz
Produced by the Canadian Centre for Architecture

143   fierce contestations over homeless encampments. Brown, who was portrayed in the national media as "Lady Gaga's ex-model," embodies the life-and-death emergency that is homelessness in America. With average life-expectancy rates that rival the world's so-called failed states—forty-eight years for an unhoused woman and fifty-one years for an unhoused man—Angelenos experiencing homelessness are disproportionately Black, heavily policed, and subject to unrelenting criminalization by propertied interests, such as business-improvement districts. While cities such as Los Angeles imposed "safer-at-home" orders to protect life during the COVID-19 pandemic, the unhoused remain abandoned, excluded from state and social protection.

The Ritz-Carlton occupation, part of a statewide No Vacancy! California campaign, drew attention to another dimension of emergency: the relationship between state power and private property. Fed up with the slow progress of Project Roomkey, a program that utilizes vacant hotel and motel rooms as emergency shelter for the unhoused, activists demanded the commandeering of hotels. They focused on "publicly subsidized" hotels, such as the Ritz-Carlton, that have benefited from tax rebates, land assembly, and many other such "geobribes," Neil Smith's felicitous phrase for the public subsidies provided by local governments to landed interests in order to facilitate urban development.[5] Just in downtown Los Angeles, public subsidies to luxury hotel development have amounted to one billion US dollars between 2005 and 2018. When housing-justice movements demand that hotels be seized to shelter the unhoused, they are seeking redress and reparation for such diversions of public money.

Commandeering is not only a political demand but also the vocabulary of legal reason. Early on in the COVID-19 shutdown, the law firm of Munger, Tolles & Olson LLP delivered a definitive legal argument stating that the mayor of Los Angeles had "broad authority" to commandeer property, including hotel rooms, "to protect public health in a declared emergency … without providing preseizure notice, an opportunity to be heard, or compensation," as long as a "post-deprivation process" provided "just compensation." A few days later, the city attorney of San Francisco arrived at a similar legal conclusion. While, to date, no government executive

5   Neil Smith, "New Globalism, New Urbanism: Gentrification as Global Urban Strategy," Antipode, vol. 34, no. 3 (2002).

in California has deployed such authority, these legal statements linger as a haunting, gesturing at the possible interruption of established relationships between state power and property rights.

The emergency that is recognized in these legal declarations is not the takings of life under conditions of global racial capitalism. The relevant emergency is public health, which has long been a key domain for governments to manage class and race relations through the management of disease. The roots of modern urban planning lie in efforts to hold the line against the spread of diseases, such as cholera, through various forms of spatial segregation and social exclusion.[6] While such practices were perfected in colonial settings where maintaining "the sanitary city" required containing and quarantining native populations,[7] they persist in what I call the postcolonial state.[8] Colonial logics of rule and subordination proliferate in and through the postcolonial state, vividly apparent in how disease is racialized and space is controlled.

Does the public health emergency at hand interrupt or consolidate such logics? On September 1, 2020, as eviction courts were set to reopen in states such as California, the Centers for Disease Control and Prevention (CDC), citing health risks, announced a nationwide moratorium on evictions, an order that supersedes local measures that "do not meet or exceed these minimum protections" and imposes criminal penalties on those violating the moratorium. While similar state-level eviction moratoria have faced legal challenges, the courts have repeatedly ruled that a halt on evictions does not violate the Takings Clause of the Fifth Amendment. For the moment, the CDC moratorium stands as an example of the police power of the state mobilized to protect human life rather than property. The moratorium is temporary, but well after the emergency is over, such an eviction ban could linger as a haunting. It could become insurgent ground.

6   As scholars like Paul Rabinow and Susan Craddock have shown in their
        works: Susan Craddock, *City of Plagues: Disease, Poverty, and Deviance in
        San Francisco* (Minneapolis: University of Minnesota Press, 2000); and Paul
        Rabinow, *French Modern: Norms and Forms of the Social Environment* (Chicago:
        University of Chicago Press, 1989).
7   Colin McFarlane, "Governing the Contaminated City: Infrastructure and Sanitation
        in Colonial and Post-colonial Bombay," *International Journal of Urban and Regional
        Research*, vol. 32, no. 2 (2008).
8   In keeping with Saidiya Hartman's work on the "afterlife of slavery," I intend the
        postcolonial as the afterlife of colonialism, rather than after-colonialism. Saidiya
        Hartman, *Lose Your Mother: A Journey Along the Atlantic Slave Route* (New York: Farrar,
        Straus & Giroux, 2007).

LOS ANGELES **USA**

MICHAEL MCCARTHY
Welder

But it's always about loss.

147　Integral to the making of insurgent ground is a practice of space, what Saidiya Hartman calls "waywardness." In Wayward Lives, Beautiful Experiments, one of the most important books of our time, she describes the long arc of Black freedom, foregrounding the lives of young Black women who "struggled to create autonomous and beautiful lives" through "open rebellion."[9] Along similar lines, Salwa Ismail argues that behind the spectacular occupations of plazas and squares of the Arab Spring was the prolonged emergency wrought by impoverished livelihoods, precarious housing, and intensifying policing. These oppressions and grievances took shape in the informal neighborhoods of cities such as Cairo, "in the microprocesses of everyday life," creating "oppositional subjectivities" and "infrastructures of protest."[10]

Such also has been the making of insurgent ground in Los Angeles. Take, for example, the People's City Council LA and People's Budget LA, emergent structures of popular sovereignty that demand the defunding of police and "a budget centered on humanity." Coalitions of racial justice and housing justice movements are rooted in long-standing struggles over redevelopment, gentrification, and policing, and now stand as a powerful challenge to the governing of/through crisis.

Yet another beautiful experiment is the popular appropriation of eminent domain, or the police power of the state to expropriate private property for public purpose. In El Sereno, the group Reclaiming Our Homes has occupied vacant houses that were acquired through eminent domain by Caltrans, California's transportation agency, for a freeway that was never built. The COVID-19 pandemic led the editorial board of the Los Angeles Times to argue for such use of property: "The state cannot allow its own vacant houses or other public properties to sit unused and crumbling in a housing and public health emergency." The editorial board went on to state: "Are the 'reclaimers' breaking the law? Of course. They're trespassing on state-owned land and, essentially, claiming public property as their own."

9　　Saidiya Hartman, Wayward Lives, Beautiful Experiments: Intimate Histories of Social Upheaval (New York: Norton, 2019).
10　　Salwa Ismail, "Urban Subalterns in the Arab Revolutions: Cairo and Damascus in Comparative Perspective," Comparative Studies in Society and History, vol. 55, no. 4 (2013).

Housing-justice movements refuse such frames of illegal occupation. They instead ask, "What is this state-owned/stolen land
on which unhoused people are trespassers? What is the law of
the postcolonial state that upholds the rights of settlement and
enforces the rightlessness of the dispossessed?" Organized theft
has been legitimized through the protocols of market rationality,
masking the forced removals of people of color as the improvement
of property value in gentrifying neighborhoods. Unrecognizable
dispossession is the prolonged state of emergency that is racial
capitalism.

If property is the insurgent ground of emergency urbanism, then
such insurgency is, perhaps, most evident in the political demand
of rent cancellation. Tracy Jeanne Rosenthal, organizer with the Los
Angeles Tenants Union, notes that most rent relief funds are "pass-
throughs for money that ends up in landlords' pockets" rather
than entitlements. By contrast, rent cancellation "would rewrite
the script of power relations." A rent strike, then, is more than the
withholding of payment. It is a political demand for the protection of
human life over the protection of property.

While Dennis Block, LA's infamous eviction attorney, argues that a
moratorium on evictions constitutes "legal theft" from landlords,
sanctioned by state power, the LA Tenants Union responds that
rent itself is theft. They invoke the dire emergency of life and death
for which housing is "the only prescription." Such are the capacious
imaginations of emergency urbanism. In the strange articulations
of crisis and uprising, an open rebellion is taking place against the
meaning of property as it has been established in the afterlife of
colonialism and slavery.

This text is a contribution of the author to the symposium
Crises Cities, co-organized by Public Books and the NYU Cities
Collaborative: https://www.publicbooks.org/emergency-
urbanism/#fn-39563-4, last accessed August 23, 2021.

Anke Butscher, Bárbara Calderón Gómez-Tejedor, Doris Kleilein, and Friederike Meyer

An Economy for the Common Good at the Local Level

A Conversation about New Values in Urban Development

151 The movement promoting an economy for the common good began in Vienna in 2010. Using a holistic and value-focused approach, and with a view to social, political, and economic issues, it champions a democratic economic system that is both socially and ecologically sustainable.[1] Anke Butscher and Bárbara Calderón Gómez-Tejedor are key figures in this movement. In Germany and Spain they advise and monitor companies, municipalities, and organizations in their accounting processes.

Ms. Butscher and Ms. Calderón Gómez-Tejedor, since the 1990s the idea of an economy for the common good has consistently been a topic of conversation as an alternative economic model. How do you understand the concept?

Anke Butscher: The common good economy is a social movement. From its point of view, economic success should not be measured purely on the basis of financial results or balance sheets but rather on the basis of the contribution an organization makes to the common good. There is thus a focus on management practices that place people and nature at the center, not growth and profit. The movement thus also appeals to Article 1 of the German constitution as an anchor for the principle that the highest goal of economic activity should be the pursuit of the common good. For me personally, common good economy means considering sustainability in terms of value, since sustainability is frequently brought up in purely ecological contexts but not in others. Moreover, I think that we can better speak to and reach people by talking about values rather than through the very elastic concept of sustainability.

Bárbara Calderón Gómez-Tejedor: I agree. The common good economy respects rights such as human dignity, solidarity, participation, and transparency, and likewise pays heed to nature. It encourages people to exercise these rights, which also contributes to their sense of autonomy. Along these lines, the goal is for members of the community to actively collaborate in constructing an inclusive and participatory framework for public policy. City administrations make decisions, for example, in response to the needs

1 According to the Gemeinwohl-Ökonomie Deutschland e.V. the common-good-economy movement is based on the ideas of the Austrian writer and journalist Christian Felber. Around 11,000 supporters worldwide have now joined the movement. Among those, roughly 5,000 are active in 200 regional groups, 800 businesses and other organizations, as well as 60 communities and cities and 200 universities. Since 2018 the International Federation of Organizations for the Common Good has been headquartered in Hamburg.

of the people they affect, communicating them either through
consultation with the public or through initiatives.

How is this fundamental approach measured and how can it
be applied to different sectors of society?

AB: The core tool is a balance sheet that takes stock of the impact
on the common good. It needs to render the contributions an
organization makes to the common good in a form that can be both
visualized and assessed; at the same time, it needs to be conducive
to the ethical development of the organization. The accounting
can be done by private companies and by other organizations,
by municipal authorities or educational institutions, for instance.
Looking forward, the common good economy aims to enlist support for a compulsory accounting process bound to specific legal
provisions, for example, in the form of tax incentives, preferential
treatment in the awarding of contracts, or favorable credit terms.
Through such strategies, the movement hopes to achieve leverage
for pursuing economic policies that consistently support organizations committed to the common good and to sustainable economic
activity overall.

Ms. Butscher, you advise, among other entities, municipal
governments in Germany in their accounting processes. Bor-
delum, Breklum, and Klixbüll in North Frisia count among the
first authorities to have prepared a common good accounting.
Why these places in particular?

AB: The municipal governments in northern Germany submitted
to the accounting process because key players in the common
good economy in this region actively approached the authorities,
who in turn seized the opportunity. The accounting of the three
municipalities has had a strong impact throughout the region.
Indeed, the district of North Frisia has passed a resolution establishing sustainability as a strategic goal and the common good
economy as a guiding policy for the region. I think that the regional
approach is crucial, since relevant issues such as sustainable
mobility or the provision of amenities such as swimming pools, can
only be addressed through a collaborative effort.

AB: A municipal authority is the state entity, in the form of a regional administrative body governed by public law, that stands closest to the people. According to the German constitution, is it as such committed to the common good. Municipalities are economic actors as well as shapers of normative frameworks and social space. They are the site where the needs and the potential of residents, businesses, and organizations flow together. Moreover, they bear responsibility for ensuring the social and ecological quality of life and the provision of public services. Based on this understanding of a municipal authority, I analyze and evaluate economic and administrative practices with municipal officials and elected representatives. We focus above all on how well they establish parameters for the common good and involve the broader society. I look to see which criteria underlie decision-making and whether these truly serve the common good—both within and beyond the borders of a municipality—or whether "practical constraints" or criteria of profitability are in fact guiding policy.

How does the accounting process play out in practical terms?

AB: The accounting takes place in workshops. As a first step, the representatives from the municipality have the opportunity to speak on the various topics. They analyze their procurement practices according to ethical criteria and assume responsibility for the upstream value chain. They observe their financial management and inquire about how to deploy their financial resources sustainably. In dealing with coworkers and elected officials, as well as volunteers who are integrated into the process, values such as the rights to freedom from bodily harm, freedom of personal development, and equality are fundamental. The municipal government reflects on its relationships to its citizens and scrutinizes whether the services it provides are geared toward social and ecological criteria. Not least, it concerns itself with whether its activities make sense for the social environment: in neighboring communities, in the region, in the state, and in the nation, as well as for future generations.

In a second step, the municipality directs its attention to what it already accomplishes in this area. Each municipality has a different set of principles guiding its decisions and evaluates its interventions differently. Those of Klixbüll in Schleswig-Holstein and Kirchanschöring in Bavaria, for example, examine the resolutions of their local councils with a view to whether they are fulfilling the criteria of a common good economy. This type of value-orientation has an impact on the budget and thus on particular areas of focus. Willebadessen in North Rhine-Westphalia, on the other hand, reviews all expenditures in light of their impact on youth and children.

In a third step, the municipality considers which benchmarks it would like to measure its activities against in the future and the actions that could be taken to achieve its goals. Thus begins a learning process that helps further motivate those who work for the municipal government, whether as full-time employees or volunteers, to pursue the common good, while also creating a compass for the future strategy. At the end, the process yields a report representing the individual values the municipality wants to realize through its actions, how it implements these values in practice, how it uses these values to assess its progress, and what potential for improvement it sees and would like to realize. Ideally, I continue to advise the municipality after the accounting as well.

Existing patterns of thinking also certainly come under scrutiny during the workshops. What do you observe there?

AB: We talk, for example, about the competition between the municipalities and the regions and about silo mentality, which is to say the purely technical kind of territorial thinking that confines itself to one area, or we talk about fears that might be prompted by community members and their demands for participation. We are seeing that many good decisions are being made but that their implementation often falls short. Ultimately, what matters is the extent to which the municipalities understand themselves to be important actors in a social-ecological transformation.

What desires and problems do you encounter in the municipalities in which you work?

AB: In the last few years, ever more official duties have devolved to the municipalities. At the same time, there has not been a corresponding increase in the number of positions created in the administration; in fact, they are more likely to have been eliminated. Municipalities in rural areas must furthermore contend with the difficulty of recruiting staff in the face of a shortage of skilled workers; positions frequently remain unfilled for lengthy periods. Municipal administrations have so many tasks to perform that they are not always enthusiastic when a new responsibility places further demands on staff resources and time. At the same time there are inertial tendencies and a certain aversion to deviating from customary and well-practiced procedures. Moreover, there is a lack of competencies with respect to sustainability, for example, in sustainable public procurement. The tendering processes must conform to certain regulatory requirements, which must follow established procedures. By now it is legally possible to implement ecological and social principles for different products and product categories, but often the knowledge about corresponding certifications or criteria catalogs is missing.

The administrative arm of municipal self-governance principally performs the function of executing tasks. But it is the political representatives who, generally across party lines, must approve decisions concerning common values and criteria for sustainability. Unfortunately, this quite often proves too difficult. There are, however, many employees in the administration who possess an intrinsic motivation to realize, in their own fields of competency, a sustainable vision and its values to the greatest extent possible. They feel encouraged by their work. Municipal action resembles a patchwork rug composed of issues, plans for intervention, and resolutions. The common good economy provides an umbrella and can activate a municipality's strategic orientation, fulfilling the wishes of many staff members.

Is the COVID-19 pandemic altering the ways the municipalities think and act?

AB: Many municipalities are currently occupied with implementing constantly changing regulations to protect against infection and the switchover to digital operations. This is not a task for which they were prepared. I think that this will precipitate a rethink of how they operate. Administration is usually organized hierarchically, but this paradigm is breaking apart, and the compulsion to control things is disappearing. Moreover, a drop in tax revenue is in the offing, which will impact municipal budgets. Administrations will

have to redetermine the criteria they use to distribute resources.
At the same time, they are asking themselves how they can better tackle future challenges. This is where the common good economy can offer answers.

What is currently propelling the movement's growth?

AB: More and more private citizens, members of the community, are becoming involved in the common good economy; they see that a social-ecological transformation is urgently needed. Many of these people are also active in their municipalities, either in political parties, initiatives, or associations, and are placing the issue of the common good on the political agenda. Administrative offices in the municipalities are also engaging with the common good economy. They are directly affected by social dislocation and the effects of climate change and see the necessity of taking action.

Ms. Calderón Gómez-Tejedor, you work in Spain by applying the fundamental principles of the common good economy. How widespread is the movement among municipal governments there?

BG: The first balance sheet was drawn up in 2014 in Miranda de Azán, a municipality in the province of Salamanca with around 400 inhabitants. In 2021, the first participatory phase was completed in Miranda de Azán and similar processes will be developed in other municipalities.

Since then, balance sheets have been prepared above all in small and medium-sized municipalities, most recently in 2020 in Guarromán, in the province of Jaén, with about 2,800 residents. In 2016, an accounting process was completed for Horta-Guinardó, a district of Barcelona with 170,000 residents. All city employees were involved in the work. Two years later, ten companies in the district followed with a total of around 2,000 employees.

In addition to municipal accounting reports, the movement in Spain also works with municipal councils to integrate the values of the common good economy in different areas. The work here is focused on local businesses and stores, and on education, for example. Through participatory processes, we identify priorities of community members, which we use to create a community common good index.

We also work closely with some regional governments. The building process "Tenerife, Island of the Common Good" with the Department of Sustainability of the Cabildo de Tenerife, the island's government, is worth highlighting.[2] This collaboration is promoting the development of the common good in three different phases: with companies, with municipalities, and finally with the island as a whole. The process is primarily about public awareness and participation of community members. It is still at an early stage, but the potential is huge.

Also noteworthy is the support to the economy for the common good that the Community of Valencia has been providing for several years through its Ministry of Sustainable Economy, Productive Sectors, Trade and Labor.[3] This is creating advantageous conditions for the shift toward an economy that has a positive impact on people and the planet. The ministry has also helped establish a chair of common good economics at the University of Valencia to promote research and training.

How is the common good economy changing urban development?

AB: Municipalities should proactively involve their residents in strategy and planning, not as token participation, but in an open process. The common good economy works here with the concept of convents or democratic assemblies. Here, the people are seen as the sovereign. However, they in turn must learn and practice to stand up for the whole and not just for their own and particular interests. Municipal urban planners should design open processes, which might of course take longer but produce results that are more effective and aligned with these principles.

2   "Tenerife, Isla del Bien Común," http://www.medioambientecabildodetenerife.es/economia-y-empleo-verdes/tenerife-isla-del-bien-comun/, last accessed May 15, 2021.
3   *La Economía del Bien Común*, video, 17:14 minutes, http://www.indi.gva.es/es/web/economia/economia-del-be-comu, last accessed May 15, 2021.

BG: Cooperation between community members and the local government is crucial. The aim must be an intergenerational dialog in which the voice of children and young people, as well as that of older people, is given greater consideration. Urban planners play an essential role in this process. Urban planning must work hand in hand with community members to build the social and cultural capital that cities need to meet the challenges of the future. And to do so, we must be guided by universal values. For example, in Miranda de Azán a few years ago, a consultation process indicated that a certain weeping willow tree held highly symbolic value for the community; it was a part of the landscape with which many people associated essential moments in their life. This awareness subsequently determined urban-planning decisions of the city council. Something similar happened with 400-year-old olive trees in the Horta-Guinardó district of Barcelona, which had to be moved to another location. After the former neighbors realized that the trees in their new location were in danger, they requested their return. The design of squares, streets, and parks determines the relationships that are created in public spaces and needs to be characterized by respect and care of a community.

Ms. Calderón Gómez-Tejedor, what is the long-term impact of your work? Can you outline this using the example of the Horta-Guinardó district in Barcelona that you mentioned earlier?

BG: Horta-Guinardó is the third largest district in Barcelona, with an area of 1,192 hectares and about 170,000 residents. The administration employs one-hundred internal and one-hundred external employees. The 2016 review was a very positive experience for everyone and an opportunity to examine with all employees how they were working. Everyone was convinced of the values of the common good economy, and groups were formed to improve community management in accordance with these values. This had an impact, for example, on contracting practices for external services. Over the years, it has been noticed that there are more and more projects that are in line with these values, such as urban gardening. There has also been great progress in terms of environmentally friendly mobility. In municipal action, the "how" is just as important as the "what." This value-based management culture is now also influencing the city council, which has set up a project group. As part of a survey, five core values were identified among all city employees: service to the community, transparency and clarity, friendliness, coproduction, and agility. The administration's decisions are now based on a set of values with enormous economic, social, and environmental impacts, for example, in the awarding of the city's sanitation service, the most important contract the city council tenders. We are talking about 2.5 billion euros over ten years. This contract allows the City Council to work with more sustainable equipment than in previous years. District manager Eduard Vicente Gómez believes it is important to integrate value-based management in the area of urban planning. Barcelona even has an urban ecology department that combines urban planning, mobility, and the environment. This department is where projects for low-emission zones, a well-maintained school environment, the promotion of electric bicycles, or the sanitation contract that I just mentioned are being created. Gómez, who led the creation of the common good balance sheet, also believes that the values of the common good economy can have a significant impact on life in major cities. He proposes that European capitals and cities join together in a common good network.

In Crisis Mode

Challenges for Hospital Planning

In response to overburdened hospital intensive care units, an international task force involving Carlo Ratti Associati, Italo Rota & Partners, Philips, and UniCredit developed the CURA emergency unit within four weeks. It consists of a converted overseas container with two beds and two setups of ICU equipment. Twenty units were installed in April 2020 in a temporary hospital located in a former industrial hall of the Turin OGR cultural center.
Image: CURApods.org

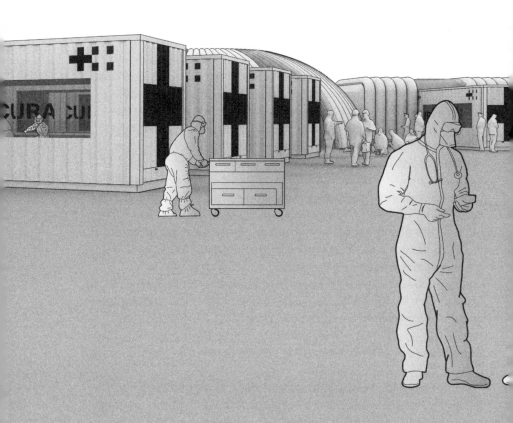

Wuhan, Madrid, New York–the images from March 2020 of over-crowded hospitals, exhausted doctors and nurses, emergency lights, and stacks of coffins made for scenes that we once knew only from science fiction movies. The daily news was defined by the rising numbers of infected and dead, and by reports of hospitals lacking sufficient protective equipment, beds, and staff. The speed with which the novel coronavirus spread in some regions, pushing up against the limits of their healthcare systems, put the entire world on alert. Its aggressive nature required intensive medical interventions for many of those afflicted; at the same time, because the risk of infection is highest prior to the emergence of symptoms, the world was forced to question its lifestyle habits and daily routines. Countries closed their borders and capped flights, imposed curfews, closed schools, and generally brought public life to a halt. Nobody knew exactly how many sick people we would have to brace ourselves for.

Crisis Management in the Exhibition Hall

Some cities reacted to the crisis with precautionary building measures to secure extra space. The fear of not being able to care for all the infected patients hastened political decisions and mobilized substantial funds for infrastructure in a minimum of time. While hospital rooms were built in Wuhan on a major construction site at warp speed, and military hospital ships dropped anchor in New York and Los Angeles to serve the general population, field hospitals took shape in soccer stadiums and parks around the world at the same time that municipal buildings and hotels were adapted for quarantine and emergency care. Some sites were intended for those suffering from mild to moderate cases of COVID-19, while others were also meant to serve as temporary overflow quarters to help sustain normal operations in the hospitals. In many cities, members of the military or various civic protection services equipped empty exhibition centers with medical devices. As an example, it only took nine days to transform the ExCel convention center in London into a 4,000-bed crisis center for the National Health Service. In the IFEMA exhibition hall in Madrid it barely took three days for 1,350 beds to be set up and connected to ventilators.

The city of Berlin also opened up an emergency hospital in its exhibition hall grounds, even though the COVID-19 numbers at the end of March 2020 were relatively low and the number of hospital beds relative to the population in Germany places it among the best worldwide. The Berlin senate allocated 40 million euros and commissioned Albrecht Broemme, a seasoned disaster management specialist and former head of the Berlin fire department, with coordinating the efforts. The reasons for the site were the same as those in other cities. For one, the exhibition centers fall within the purview of the municipal authority, and their regular operations had been shut down due to the pandemic. For another, the grounds are well connected logistically and the facilities well equipped and ventilated; moreover, there are no neighbors who could object to the choice of site. The fundamental design, courtesy of Heinle, Wischer und Partner, an architectural firm well-versed in hospital construction, was developed over a single weekend as a cluster structure based on the intensive care bed—the smallest unit of hospital planning.[1] Broemme's team needed only four weeks to complete the building. Within four weeks sound-insulation coatings were applied to 12,000 square meters of concrete flooring; subsequently, walls were erected, pipes laid, and 500 beds and ventilators installed. Decisions that would normally require a week were made within ten minutes, and the technical approvals for issues relating to hygiene, fire protection, and workplace safety occurred in comparatively minimal time and yet still at the usual high level demanded by hospitals.[2] All those involved, including the famously sluggish authorities in Berlin, made tremendous accomplishments in crisis mode.

One year after the beginning of the pandemic, in the spring of 2021, the use value of these infrastructure measures appears sobering, at least in the Western world. Apart from Madrid, where 4,000 people were treated within 41 days, and the tent hospital in New York's central park, where 191 mild cases were treated during just a few weeks, the emergency medical treatment centers that were set up remained significantly underutilized. Nobody has been treated in the Berlin facility so far; the emergency hospital is solely used for trainings and is to remain open and ready for operation, with it ultimately being disassembled by September 2021. The auxiliary hospital on the exhibition grounds in Hannover, where 70,000 square meters was cleared for 485 beds, has likewise not yet been put to use. The building offensive undertaken by the British government,

1   Edzard Schultz, partner at Heinle, Wischer und Partner, Independent Architects, March 16, 2021, conversation with the author.
2   Ibid.

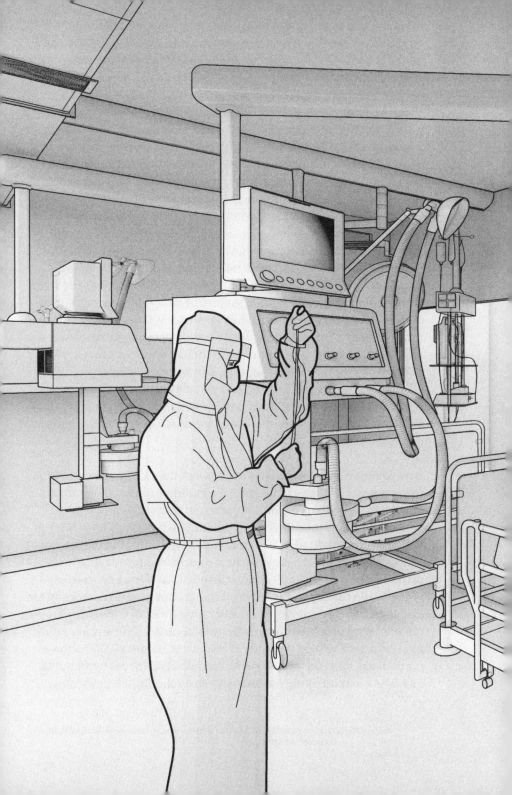

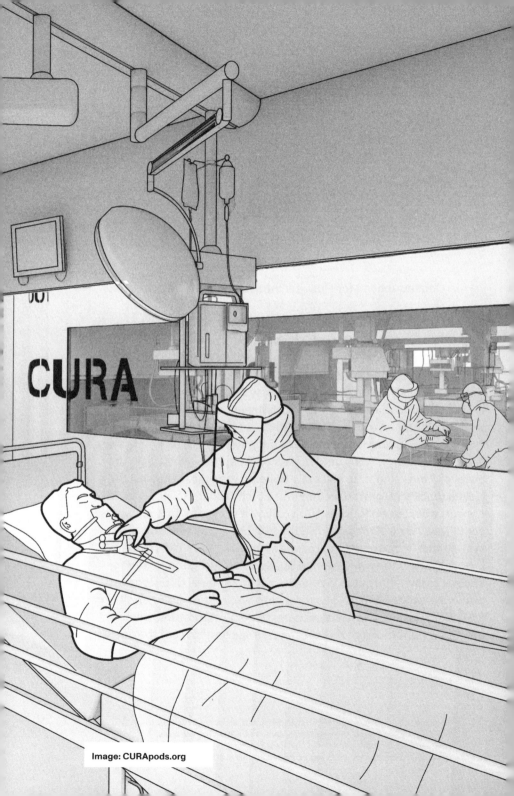

Image: CURApods.org

which had invested more than 532 million pounds in several pop-up treatment centers across the country, also turned out in retrospect to have been excessive. Fifty-four people were treated in London; a mere four weeks later, the facility was closed due to a lack of demand. During the first wave around one-hundred cases were treated in Manchester and twenty-nine in Exeter; Birmingham and Sunderland had no admissions. On the one hand, one can view the emergency centers as a political failure, an attempt during a crisis to use large sums of money to combat structural deficits.[3] On the other hand, at the time they were built, they seemed to be an appropriate strategy for managing the crisis, as they ensured the provision of constitutionally guaranteed essential public services by making well-functioning hospitals available to the population.

Consequences for Hospital Infrastructure in Germany

But while the local authorities were setting up emergency hospitals or having new ones built, news reports from the care wards showed that managing the pandemic was only partly a question of building infrastructure. In the West, Germany included, it quickly became clear that the strain on the healthcare system had less to do with spatial circumstances and more with the initial lack of protective equipment and an overburdened staff. (It should be noted, however, that the latter circumstance was nothing new.) Will the emergency centers, auxiliary clinics, and makeshift hospitals go down in the history of the pandemic as costly building measures that will be just as quickly forgotten as they were built, and that were unable to prevent a number of nurses from calling it quits due to poor working conditions? Or will they prompt the building up of a healthcare system that is better able to manage future crises? The pandemic is posing anew the fundamental question of how good health for all can remain affordable. Even when sociopolitical decisions are primarily responsible for ensuring improvement of staff conditions and general access to medical care, built infrastructure, which is the paramount focus of this text, is an important part of the answer.

3   Susanna Rustin, "The Empty Nightingale Hospitals Show the Cost of Putting Buildings before People," *The Guardian*, January 27, 2021, https://www. theguardian.com/commentisfree/2021/jan/27/empty-nightingale-hospitals-government-healthcare-staff, last accessed August 4, 2021.

A healthcare system that can flexibly react to special situations and at the same time make the profession of nursing more attractive will have to accord a greater importance to infection protection than it has in the past. In recent decades, chronic illnesses, the bodily consequences of prosperity, and the promise of a long life were the chief forces that presented challenges for the provision of healthcare and furthered the development of hospitals. Hospitals today are compact facilities whose built structures must be adapted to new treatment methods and technical devices. Many buildings claim to engender an atmosphere that supports the healing process and offers staff a pleasant working environment, but the economic pressure is enormous. Again and again, staff must seek a balance between costs incurred, medical usefulness, and the ethical demands of medicine. A system designed for economic efficiency is not prepared for a pandemic—neither for the risk of infection nor for the many people who become sick at the same time.

Since the middle of the twentieth century, medicine had become increasingly convinced that the lethal threat of infectious diseases had been vanquished. According to Petra Gastmeier, a specialist in hygiene and environmental medicine at the Charité hospital in Berlin, the role of infectious diseases in the public sphere receded with the discovery of penicillin by Alexander Fleming. Positions for infectious diseases at universities were no longer filled. In 1967, the American doctor William H. Stewart was even tempted to claim that the time had come to declare the end of the battle against infectious diseases. Cost savings necessitated by the oil crisis of the 1970s even had an impact on the building of hospitals; among other things, these cuts dislodged the important design criterion of preventing infection. Many internal spaces were created, and ventilation systems were altered in favor of circulated air, drawing less fresh air. [4] Many of these spatial conditions still exist today.

Even when specialist media for architecture currently conveys a different impression, new construction is relatively infrequent for hospitals in Germany. The task of hospital planning concerns much

4   See Petra Gastmeier, "Bauliche Infektionsprävention im Gebäude," lecture in the series "Zukunft Bau: Perspektiven für das Bauen im Wandel," Studio Bund, online, January 15, 2021, beginning at minute 24:00, https://www.zukunftbau.de/veranstaltungen/bau-2021/rueckblick, last accessed May 8, 2021.

more the development and modernization of existing structures.
Thirty-five percent of hospitals in Germany were built between 1961 and 1990, 23 percent between 1901 and 1945. Half of the total stock includes structures that have grown into their current form, as their building parts were added to each other over time.[5]

Stewart's statement has long since proven to be a misjudgment. Recent years have seen an increase in outbreaks of new infectious diseases.[6] COVID-19 is not the first novel virus, nor will it be the last. The coming years will see new pathogens that can be traced, as with SARS-Cov-2, back to animal-to-human transmission. Then there is the rising risk of resistant hospital germs. There are already around half a million patients in Germany every year who acquire infections during their hospitals stays.[7] It is assumed that these infections cause around 10,000 to 15,000 patient deaths every year in Germany.[8] Research into infection protection within buildings has as a result been intensified. These issues have drawn increased attention due to the pandemic.

In 2019, there were 1,914 hospitals with 494,000 patient beds nationwide.[9] That means roughly 1,900 hospitals will need to prepare for future occurrences of infection by unknown pathogens. For architecture, this means, above all, a need to remain or become flexible. Flexibility is crucial, since not all pathogens are transmitted in the same way, and not all are equally aggressive. According to the architect Wolfgang Sunder, coordinator of several inter-disciplinary studies of infection-mitigation strategies in the built environment, when tackling a new infectious disease it is important to quickly and efficiently acquire scientific insight into possible routes of transmission and to interrupt these routes with archi-tectural, spatial, and technological measures.[10] The development

---

5   See Wolfgang Sunder et al., *Das Patientenzimmer: Planung und Gestaltung* (Basel: Birkhäuser, 2021): 165, 166.
6   See German Bundestag, Wissenschaftliche Dienste, January 12, 2021, "Sachstand Zoonosen, Pandemiepotential," https://www.bundestag.de/resource/blob/819242/5292551d2d6408842537ac1ee76dd8e6/WD-9-110-20-pdf-data.pdf, last accessed June 24, 2021.
7   See Wolfgang Sunder et al., "Bauliche Hygiene im Klinikbau, Planungsempfehlungen für die bauliche Infektionsprävention in den Bereichen der Operation, Notfall- und Intensivmedizin," published by the Federal Institute for Research on Building, Urban Affairs and Spatial Development (BBSR) (Bonn, 2020): 5.
8   See Petra Gastmeier and Christine Geffers, "Nosokomiale Infektionen in Deutschland," *Deutsche Medizinische Wochenschrift* 133 (2008): 1111–1115.
9   See *Bundesärzteblatt*, March 1, 2021. From a response by the Federal Ministry of Health to a question from the Left Party, https://www.aerzteblatt.de/nachrichten/121611/Strukturwandel-Bettenabbau-in-den-Krankenhaeusern, last accessed March 19, 2021.

of solutions for the improved management and combating of the pandemic is thus not reserved solely for one group of specialists; it demands the participation of experts from entirely different disciplines and fields.[11] Along with the discussion of ventilation systems, the call for more single rooms in hospitals has gotten louder since the beginning of the pandemic. And yet, as Sunder says, just as CO_2 emissions cannot be reduced to zero overnight, four-bed rooms cannot suddenly be transformed into singles.[12] According to an inquiry in 2015, 44.4 percent of the rooms in the general wards of German hospitals contain more than two beds.[13] The urgency of this matter is confirmed by the passage of a federal bill in October 2020, the Hospital Future Act, which allocates money for purposes such as emergency departments and patient rooms, providing them with improved information technology and technical equipment.[14]

But infection protection in buildings has long ceased to be simply a matter of the number of rooms and high-performance technical fixtures. It starts with apparently small details such as the correct placement of disinfectant dispensers, and includes the choice of surface materials for the room furniture and the installation of double door systems as well as the question of how to organize the intake process at the hospital's emergency room.[15] Along with the selection of materials and spatial organization, infection protection also concerns the question of accessibility and how to design spaces that intentionally influence the behavior of staff, patients, and guests.[16] At the height of the first wave of the pandemic, a study was conducted at the Mount Sinai Hospital in New York, under the direction of the MASS design group, that demonstrated just how important a role human behavior plays in these matters.

10   See BBSR, *Bauliche Hygiene im Klinikbau; Zukunft Bauen: Forschung für die Praxis*, vol. 13. Interdisciplinary research project led by Dr. Wolfgang Sunder (Institute for Industrial Construction and Structural Design at TU Braunschweig) and Prof. Petra Gastmeier (Charité Berlin), https://www.bbsr.bund.de/BBSR/DE/veroeffentlichungen/zukunft-bauen-fp/2018/band-13.html, last accessed June 24, 2021.

11   Ibid.

12   See Wolfang Sunder, March 19, 2021, conversation with the author.

13   See Sunder, *Das Patientenzimmer*, 167.

14   See Section 19.11, "Gesetz für ein Zukunftsprogramm Krankenhäuser," *German Federal Law Gazette* Part I no. 48., https://www.bundesgesundheitsministerium.de/fileadmin/Dateien/3_Downloads/Gesetze_und_Verordnungen/GuV/K/bgbl1_S.2208_KHZG_28.10.20.pdf.

15   See Sunder, conversation with author.

16   Ibid.

The study noted that up until the outbreak of the pandemic, hospitals considered people afflicted with infectious diseases as exceptions, not the norm. Risk zones within the departments were perceived in very different ways. The investigation concluded that codes of conduct needed to be infection-specific and above all clearly communicated to staff.[17] In this context, the significance of signage systems became a focal point of design. As public spaces in which new people are constantly encountering changing and sometimes emotionally challenging situations, hospitals need to offer clearly legible orientation for users, which entails particular rules of behavior. Aware that human behavior was the decisive factor for infection risk, many hospitals in crisis mode transformed themselves into fortresses in an attempt to combat the pandemic. Recovering patients could only receive encouragement from relatives over the telephone, and mourners scarcely found solace as they could not even say goodbye to the deceased.[18]

Between a Field Hospital, an Individual Container, and a Quarantine Paradise

But will bedside visits ever be allowed again in hospitals? Do we not in fact need a completely new understanding of spaces for healing and care? Even before the pandemic, predictions about the future of the German healthcare system proceeded from the assumption that staff shortages would get worse and the costs of care would rise, that more care would take place on an outpatient basis, and that there would be more specialized clinics and fewer twenty-four-hour hospitals. And yet now the weaknesses of the system are becoming ever clearer. One of the positive effects of the pandemic is the robust impulse it has given to considerations about what a hospital, or better, a place for getting healthy, can be in the future.

In search of models for a lean, cost-effective healthcare-delivery structure, observers often turn to Denmark, where for many years inpatient treatment has been cut back in favor of outpatient care. In 2007 the Danish government passed a 5.5 billion euro master plan to support the conversion of the medical care system's building

17   See Ariadne Labs, MASS Design Group (n.d.), "Role of Architecture in Fighting COVID-19," https://massdesigngroup.org/covidresponse, last accessed March 28, 2021.
18   See *76 Days* (2000), documentary by Hao Wu, Weixi Chen, and an anonymous third party from the early days of the COVID-19 pandemic in the sealed-off city of Wuhan.

171 facilities into fewer, more specialized large clinics and smaller urgent care units. Admittedly, this was only possible because the hospitals in Denmark lie almost exclusively in the hands of the state.[19] In Germany, rapid, structural changes are more difficult to achieve, even if the political will were present. This is due not only to the diversity of administrative forms, from public to independent nonprofit to private, but also to complicated matters of shared jurisdiction and the fact that there is as yet no federal hospital building ordinance that supersedes those of the individual states. Where can planning come in at all?

Architects and planners have taken the pandemic as an occasion to visualize spatial ideas, thereby raising new questions. Are future spaces of convalescence more likely to be located in the middle of nature, such as the Waldklink in Eisenberg in the state of Thuringia, which sees itself as a touristic landmark and welcomes travelers passing by to stop at its restaurant? Will there be more sites for alternative medicine, where medicinal healing plants are cultivated and patients can undertake therapeutic experiments on their own? Or will hospitals be more like small cities within a city, in which the municipal government operates libraries, museums, and daycare centers in addition to providing medical care?

Many ideas indicate that spaces for curing bodily suffering could take on all kinds of forms, depending on the disease, the incidence of infection, and the financial situation of patients. If we are to succeed in giving everyone a right to basic medical care irrespective of their income, many people in the future will recover at home with telemedical care, or at least they will be forced to do so for financial reasons.[20] Some medical facilities will operate more like logistics centers, dispatching online orders via drone or sending mobile robots with personalized medications to patients' front doors.[21] Remaining within the paradigm of the crisis mode, others could be set up and taken down again like stage scenery, an idea entertained by the video *OMA Hospital of the Future (Twelve Cautionary Urban*

19   See Tobias Buschbeck and Susanne Glade, "Was ist anders in Dänemark?," *Bauwelt* 17 (Gütersloh, 2012).
20   Founded in 2015, Mercy Virtual Care Center in the Midwestern United States provides 24/7 care via screens to patients at home and in forty-three hospitals in five states with approximately 300 medical professionals.
21   The Tübingen-based biotech company Curevac has submitted a vaccine printer for approval. The mobile production facility is expected to produce mRNA vaccines starting in summer 2021. See https://www.aerztezeitung.de/Wirtschaft/Curevac-erprobt-in-Kuerze-Impfstoffdrucker-fuer-COVID-19-Vakzin-417587.html, last accessed April 18, 2021.

Tales),[22] or, like the CURA prototypes of Carlo Ratti, they could be manufactured in advance in large quantities so as to have a ready inventory of container-based isolation stations.[23] It is possible that in the future we will see a need for mobile and scalable spaces for quarantine that will realign our relationship to nature through cheerful architecture, rather than diminishing our quality of life in seclusion, just as Gustav Düsing and Carson Chan envision with full hedonism in their project Fortnightism.[24] Perhaps fixed hospital rooms for inpatient care will be increasingly indistinguishable from hotel suites; perhaps people with means will fly around the world in order to visit clinic-like installations near airports where they have parts of their bodies optimized or replaced. Or perhaps the graveyards of decommissioned planes will one day be converted into sanatoria for the treatment of lingering COVID-19 aftereffects, so-called long COVID. However, the world seeks to cope with this and future pandemics: without caregivers or an unconditional aspect to medical care for all people—and this is certainly the most important lesson to be taken from hospital planning during the pandemic—even the best place for the sick to recover will remain useless infrastructure.

22   See Hans Larsson, Alex Retegan, and Reiner de Graaf, *OMA Hospital of the Future (Twelve Cautionary Urban Tales)*, Matadero Madrid, Centre for Contemporary Creation, © OMA, https://vimeo.com/495484280, last accessed April 7, 2021.
23   See https://carloratti.com/project/cura, last accessed March 29, 2021.
24   See Niklas Maak, "Das Haus der vierzehn Nächte," *Frankfurter Allgemeine Zeitung*, November 21, 2020, 11.

Notes on the Just City

According to a report from the global emergency aid and development organization Oxfam, the coronavirus pandemic has dramatically increased inequality worldwide.[1] Global poverty is as high as it was five years ago. The gap between rich and poor—that is, between those who have fallen further behind because of the COVID-19 crisis, and those who are profiting massively from it—continues to widen. Oxfam's sober assessment: the cause of this growing inequality is an economic system that not only continues to compel and reproduce this very inequality, but that has also brought about the climate crisis by exploiting people and the planet.[2]

If the demands for a just city and a fair distribution of space have already become louder and louder in recent years, the pandemic has exacerbated them even further over the past year. But what exactly is a just city? What does justice mean when applied concretely to urban development, the use of space, or existing and emerging architecture? What does spatialized justice look like?

1   See Oxfam Deutschland e.V. (2021), "Das Ungleichheitsvirus: Wie die Corona-Pandemie soziale Ungleichheit verschärft und warum wir unsere Wirtschaft gerechter gestalten müssen," https://www.oxfam.de/system/files/documents/oxfam_factsheet_ungleichheitsvirus_deutsch.pdf, last accessed April 4, 2021.
2   Ibid.

In order to delimit his huge field, it is helpful to take a somewhat broader view, which can also be seen not least in the current climate emergency. But more on that later. First, I would like to start with questions directly addressed to those planning "our" future: who in fact are these people who have been entrusted with the planning of cities, with the design of living environments and the built future, and who will be entrusted with these tasks at a later time? who, in the words of Lucius Burckhardt, will design the planning that makes processes of design and urban development possible at all?[3] In the search for the just city, we will first have to address who is planning, for whom and with whom. This "for" or "with" points us to different approaches. The issue immediately becomes quite complex, because these approaches speak not least of a responsibility that is assumed—on whose behalf?—to shape the space in which we live. The issue also concerns responsibilities, and with whom they may be entrusted.

Societies around the world have become sensitized to these issues, and not just since the beginnings of the Occupy movement. Hardly anyone today would claim that urban development—speaking very broadly—is truly inclusive. Many of the large-scale visions of recent decades have expressed and realized the desires of the ideas—and of the excesses of power and capital—of the "few." These are visions that have not really aligned with the needs of the "many." And this led to increased talk of exclusionary urbanization processes, that is, of planning that feeds on private-sector logic without being conceived or constituted in terms of inclusivity. This is clearly visible in statistics. We can see it in the widening gap mentioned above between rich and poor. Yet even more clearly than any set of dry statics, it is the realized spaces in which we live—spaces that we know ourselves and those that are conveyed to us through images and reports—that articulate this so clearly. We all know that some people, a very small number, benefit greatly from the opportunities, money flows, and trade links that span the globe. Quite many others do not enjoy these options. But it is these global profiteers who shape spaces in their own interests (including monetary ones). Spaces thus proliferate in which we are allowed to spend time only if we pay for them. At the same time, other

3   See Lucius Burckhardt, "Who Plans the Planning?," in *Lucius Burckhardt: Writings; Rethinking Man-Made Environments: Politics, Landscape & Design*, ed. Jesko Fezer and Martin Schmitz (Vienna/New York: Springer, 2012 [1974]): 85–101.

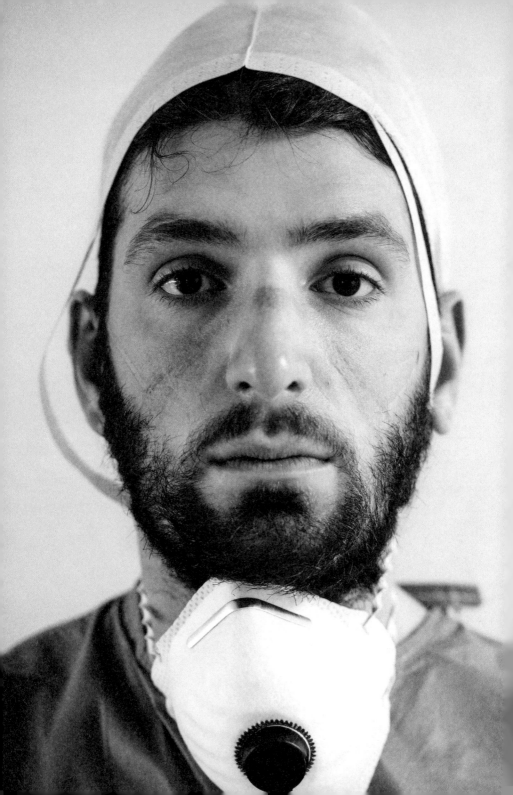

spaces—spaces that are open to the public and that can be used for free, which are the very spaces that have established themselves during the pandemic as absolutely essential places of recreation and recentering—are slowly but steadily disappearing from the scene. These "paid spaces," however, are not just proliferating. They also have a habit of crowding out the other spaces. All this happens not infrequently under the premise of "upgrading"—a seemingly innocent word for the thoroughly violent processes that come with it, but which can less and less often be disguised with these euphemistic terms. That is to say: urban structures change—sometimes slowly and insidiously, sometimes quite rapidly. And the space for those who possess little is dwindling. "Justice is some-thing else!" the choir now declaims.

One objection here, perhaps justified, is that not everything was rosy in the past either. That the processes described here are not new. That today displacement may be called gentrification, but that nothing else has changed. And yes, that may be so. But the resis-tance that is stirring, the protests, which are massive and getting louder—these are special. A city must be made differently. It must be planned, designed, built, and managed in such a way that it is not just luck, favorable circumstances, or financial resources that determine what lives are possible there. The right to the city must be absolute.

When we read books on the subject, this right is often tied to the right to clean water, clean air, housing, adequate sanitation, mobility, education, healthcare, and democratic participation in decision-making. Yet as Peter Marcuse argues, this must also be about social justice, which includes the right to individual justice but goes far beyond it.[4] We are talking here about the city as a place (once again referring to Marcuse) for a heterogeneous and complex society that offers the same opportunities to all.[5]

Even today, many who deal with these questions and thoughts refer to Henri Lefebvre, whose 1968 book about the right to the city remains so current.[6] At the time, Lefebvre's work helped formulate

4   See Peter Marcuse, "Whose Right(s) to What City?," in *Cities for People, Not for Profit: Critical Urban Theory and the Right to the City*, ed. Neil Brenner, Peter Marcuse, and Margit Mayer (New York: Routledge, 2012 [1974]): 41.
5   Ibid.
6   See Henri Lefebvre, *Le droit à la ville* (Anthropos: Paris, 1968).

a critique of capitalism and the institutionalization of life more generally—and it can still be read the same way today. But Lefebvre not only articulates criticism (another reason why this text, which is more than fifty years old, will remain relevant); at least as some read him, he also elaborates exactly how this other, this just city must be designed. The principles he mentions concern self-organization through participation, self-determination, and appropriation. They are manifestations of collective demands postulated by those who actively inhabit the city, but which must be constantly redebated and renegotiated. Often, Lefebvre says, these demands are the result of political struggles.[7]

Lefebvre outlines how the just city would have to be organized, how it would have to be managed, and perhaps even what it would have to look like. He is not concerned with an easy transformation and reformation of the apparatuses and mechanisms that drive our existing cities. Neither the state nor capitalism has a place in his model. The just city must escape the control and disciplinary mechanisms of these systems because it is underpinned by fundamentally different values. Lefebvre thus opposes the violent, exploitative, exclusionary, instrumentalizing city with another imaginarium, which almost seems to be a formless construct but is nevertheless more than just a shell. It needs to be negotiated, to be co-created, and to be inclusive without forming rigid communities.

To put it another way: justice, and justice on a spatial level, cannot be implemented by signing one, two, or more petitions from the comfort of one's own living room. The systems that make our existing cities seemingly run so smoothly also alienate and mar-ginalize—implicitly and explicitly. This has been brought home to us by the pandemic as perhaps never before. The task is to reclaim this alienated space. It is to reclaim space that has been taken away from the common good and community by neoliberalizing princi-ples and the ongoing privatization of public assets, to claim it for other social and communalized relational networks. In doing so, we cannot necessarily or unconditionally fall back on existing (state) structures. Rather, we must think, design, and implement new systems and new institutions—and not as temporary interventions, even if these may always have their usefulness and thus a certain

7   Ibid.

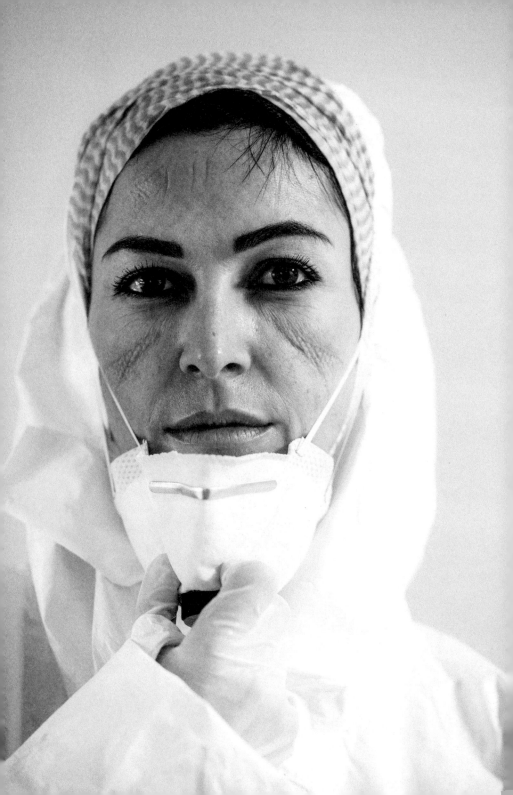

justification. On the contrary: the right to the city cannot be a traveling circus. Briefly putting up a tent, only to (hastily) leave before too many traces are left behind—this is clearly the wrong approach. It would also be wrong, in demanding other principles, to look only at the rights of individuals—not least because it is precisely this focus on the individual that has produced whatever state of emergency in which we currently find ourselves. Instead, everyone must continually fight, with more and more energy, to ensure that collective rights (to clean water, clean air, affordable housing, public space, and so on) are enshrined for the long term. Only in this way can the major challenges of our time finally be addressed with the necessary seriousness—first and foremost, the global climate emergency, which is hurtling toward us at a dizzying pace without prompting any significant political reactions.

I won't conclude by drawing up any formulas for the just city. I'm not going to present a toolbox that we could employ. Similarly, I'm not going to suggest trying out a recipe for design thinking that might seem attractively innovative. Nor do I have an exercise ready that we could use to produce readymades that would help us get out of this vexing situation. In this text, I have only obliquely touched upon the questions I posed at its outset. Quite deliberately, I have left others completely unexamined because what I am suggesting here is that we use these questions as a starting point for our own work and activities. Together with the other reflections in this volume, they can be understood as a barometer, a storm glass, perhaps even a pressure indicator. They can be used to make assessments, to point out uneven developments and design other systems.

But even if there is no simple recipe for the just city, because justice has to be negotiated in cooperation, there are nevertheless things that we can postulate in general. Here again, I take recourse to Peter Marcuse, to his claim that there can be no justice in neoliberal systems. Existing neoliberal systems and mechanisms, Marcuse argued, must be actively opposed.[8] The just city, then, must set its focus on alternatives. What does this mean for the just city? And what does that mean for the act of planning itself, if this is what it will still be called in the future? As a first step, Marcuse calls for analyzing, making visible, and communicating the roots of contemporary problems. These analyses can then be used in a

8   Vgl. Marcuse (2012) (wie Anm. 4)

second step, by all those who create space, and with the tools of critical theory, to develop other proposals. And then—which seems most important here—he repeatedly demands that we politicize, politicize, politicize.

Yet an awareness of the danger of repetition means that Marcuse's principle is of course no magic bullet either. The just city is and remains a process of negotiation; it is and remains a common project, and it can only be implemented through a great deal of effort on the part of all of us—only to continually be renegotiated, replanned, and questioned. But one thing is clear: things cannot and must not go on as they have. There is too much at stake for that.

Don't do
Produce islands no one can reach and from which one can leave; stage circus events; make common cause with exploitative systems.

Do
Join solidarity networks; think about the impact of planning on and for others; invent multiple ways of co-designing other systems; finally confront the great challenges of our time with serious proposals.

The text is a revised version of the essay "Justice" published in the anthology *Glossar zur gemeinwohlorientierten Stadtentwicklung* (edited by BBSR, 2020).

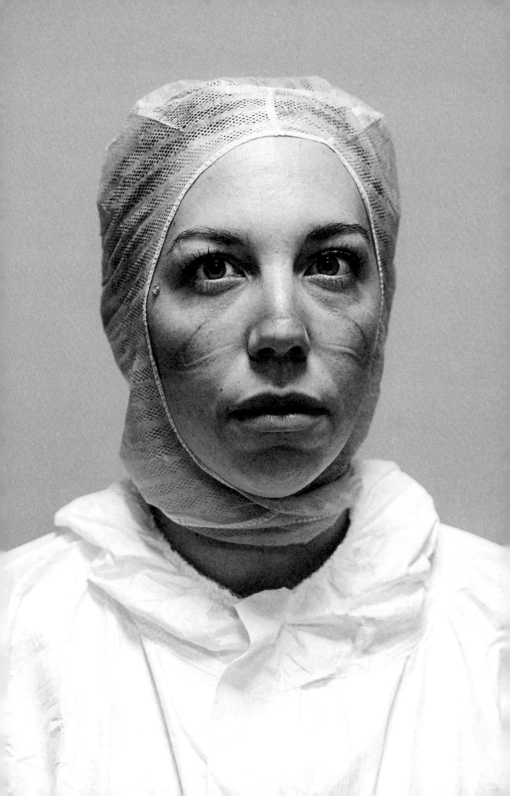

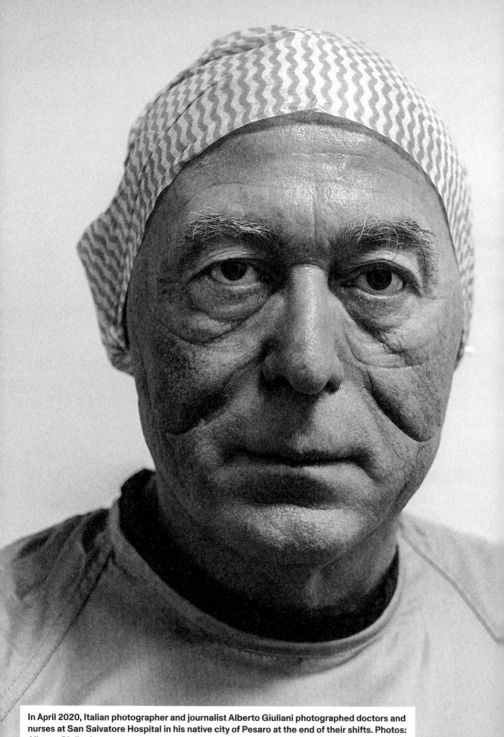

In April 2020, Italian photographer and journalist Alberto Giuliani photographed doctors and nurses at San Salvatore Hospital in his native city of Pesaro at the end of their shifts. Photos: Alberto Giuliani

Sascha Anders has been a research associate at HafenCity University Hamburg (HCU) since 2011, where his research interests include urban transformation processes.

Sabine Bauer is an architect and university assistant at the Institute of Urbanism at Graz University of Technology. Her research focuses on active mobility, design of public spaces, and development planning in periurban areas. She is currently working on spatial intervention mechanisms in the research project Tactical Mobilism and a regional strategy for the Krottendorf-Gaisfeld area.

Anke Butscher is a social scientist and economist, managing partner of corsus, and an expert on sustainability of organizations and supply chains and the common good economy. She advises companies, municipalities, and organizations on value-oriented accounting processes, and municipalities on sustainable municipal and urban development.

Bárbara Calderón Gómez-Tejedor is a specialist in sustainable development and international migration. She studied European Business Administration at the Universidad Pontificia Comillas as well at the ESB Reutlingen and is active in research and consulting for municipalities on social cohesion and the common good economy.

Aglaée Degros is professor and chair of the Institute of Urbanism at Graz University of Technology, science fellow at the Vrije Universiteit Brussel, and co-founder with Stefan Bendiks of Artgineering. She is a board member of several institutions in Austria and Belgium and serves as an advisor to ministers and cities.

Futures Probes is a research collective of four female futurists, two of whom—Katrina Günther and Elena Artiles Leyes—have also collaborated with Non Voyage. Katrina is an illustrator and lecturer for design and foresight. Elena is a political scientist, researching the potential of regenerative tourism in the Canary Islands.

Stephan Große has been a research associate at HafenCity University Hamburg (HCU) since 2018, focusing on topics that include small and medium-sized cities or rural and suburban areas.

Kerem Halbrecht is a critical spatial practitioner. He founded 72 Hour Urban Action, the world's first real-time architecture festival, and co-founded PlattenBaum which develops infrastructure for urban Aagriculture. Kerem also co-founded Non Voyage.

Phineas Harper is director of Open City and Open House Worldwide, and a columnist at *Dezeen*. In 2019 he co-curated the Oslo Architecture Triennale and the 19th Architecture Prize of the Land Steiermark. He also serves as an advisor to a cross-party suburban taskforce in the UK. Between 2015 and 2020, he was deputy director of the Architecture Foundation in London, establishing the New Architecture Writers program in collaboration with Tom Wilkinson.

Felix Hartenstein lives and works as an urban economist in Berlin. He consults, teaches, and conducts research on new forms of work in the city, the digital economy and urban development, Silicon Valley urbanism, and corporate urban responsibility, among other topics. He is co-editor of the 2017 anthology CSR & Stadtentwicklung: Unternehmen als Partner für eine Nachhaltige Stadtentwicklung.

Thomas Krüger has been a professor at HafenCity University Hamburg (HCU) since 2000, where he heads the Department of Project Development and Project Management in Urban Planning.

Markus Monsberger is an architect and project assistant at the Institute of Urbanism at Graz University of Technology. He is focusing on smart development in small and medium-sized cities and is a representative of the Institute in the Urban Mobility Laboratory Graz. At Artgineering he works on the transformation of urban spaces, especially with bicycle infrastructure.

Agnes Müller is an architect and urban researcher in Berlin. She completed a PhD on flexible work environments in urban spaces, focusing on coworking spaces. She researches and teaches on urban commons and urban mobility in the programs in urban design and urban and regional planning at the TU Berlin and coordinates the TU Berlin's dual master's program urban planning and mobility with the Universidad de Buenos Aires.

189 **Eitan Nir** is a cultural planner, social scientist, and data analyst. He co-founded e-Boded—a production company for music festivals and events. He is a member of Non Voyage.

Zachi Razel is a designer and builder working at the intersection of architecture, art, and social practice. He is a founding member of Torhaus Berlin, e.V., a community space and association for social urban projects. He is also a partner in KLAK—design & build studio. Zachi co-founded Non Voyage.

Stefan Rettich is an architect and professor of urban planning at the University of Kassel. From 2011 to 2016 he was professor of theory and design at the University of Applied Sciences Bremen, after teaching for four years at the Bauhaus Kolleg in Dessau. He is a founding partner and co-owner of KARO* architects.

Ananya Roy is professor of urban planning, social welfare, and geography and The Meyer and Renee Luskin Chair in Inequality and Democracy at the University of California, Los Angeles.

Sarah Schalk is a multimedia designer, philosopher, and physicist. She has created workshops, installations, and games in public space. She is the recipient of the Award for Movies on Human Rights in Nuremberg. She is part of Non Voyage.

Tatjana Schneider has been professor of architectural theory at TU Braunschweig since 2018. She researches, discusses, writes about, and resists violent—exploitative, speculative, and exclusionary—productions of architecture, city, and space.

David Sim is an independent urban advisor. He was trained as an architect in Scotland and Scandinavia and worked as an educator at Lund University. For ten years he was creative director at Gehl, specialized in urban design and planning, putting Jan Gehl's theories into large-scale projects all over the world.

Nat Skoczylas is a cultural worker, curator, and researcher of collective practices at the Royal Institute of Art in Stockholm. She has presented at the Biennale of Design in Ljubljana and programmed events for the Tektura squat in Lublin. She is a member of Non Voyage.

Maria Smith is director of sustainability and physics at Buro Happold. As an architect, engineer, writer, and curator she works across disciplines to bring the built environment in line with planetary limits. She is a member of the council of the Royal Institute of British Architects and a trustee of the Architecture Foundation. In 2017, she was appointed a design advocate by the Greater London Authority and 2019 as co-chief curator of the Oslo Architecture Triennale.

Philipp Stierand is a spatial planner and expert on community food policy. For more than fifteen years, he has participated as an expert in the debate on food supply in cities and regions. From 2001, he built up the natural food industry's further education institution Weiling.Akademie, which he headed until 2019. He is the managing director of Speiseräume Forschungs- und Beratungsgesellschaft and heads Berlin's Kantine Zukunft.

Doris Kleilein is an architect, author, and publisher in Berlin. In 2005, she co-founded the architectural office bromsky. From 2005 to 2018, she worked as editor of *Bauwelt* and *Stadtbauwelt*, and since 2019 has directed the publishing house JOVIS in Berlin, specialized on books in urbanism and architecture.

Friederike Meyer is a journalist and publicist. She studied architecture in Aachen and Seattle and at the Evangelische Medienakademie in Berlin. She worked as editor for *Bauwelt*, guest editor at *Hochparterre*, lecturer in architectural communication in Kaiserslautern and has been editor-in-chief at *Baunetz.de* since 2017.

The idea for this book developed during the fellowship of Doris Kleilein und Friederike Meyer at Thomas Mann House in Los Angeles 2020.

© 2021 by jovis Verlag GmbH
Texts by kind permission of the authors.
Pictures by kind permission of the photographers/
holders of the picture rights.

Cover: The Polcevera Park and the Red Circle, Genua, 2019. Design:
Stefano Boeri Architetti, Metrogramma Milano, Inside Outside |
Petra Blaisse

English translation: Michael Thomas Taylor and Benjamin R. Trivers
(pp. 7–10, 33, 34–48, 49–63, 64–71, 72–82, 83–95, 126–138, 150–159,
160–172, 173–184)
Copyediting: Michael Thomas Taylor and Benjamin R. Trivers
Design and Setting: Floyd E. Schulze
Lithography: Bild1Druck
Production: Susanne Rösler
Printed in the European Union

Bibliographic information published by the Deutsche
Nationalbibliothek.
The Deutsche Nationalbibliothek lists this publication in the Deutsche
Nationalbibliografie; detailed bibliographic data are available on the
Internet at http://dnb.d-nb.de.

jovis Verlag GmbH
Lützowstraße 33
10785 Berlin

www.jovis.de

jovis books are available worldwide in select bookstores.
Please contact your nearest bookseller or visit www.jovis.de
for information concerning your local distribution.

ISBN 978-3-86859-710-3 (English edition, softcover)
ISBN 978-3-86859-981-7 (English edition, PDF)
ISBN 978-3-86859-671-7 (German edition, softcover)
ISBN 978-3-86859-966-4 (German edition, PDF)